W9-BIN-715

J The JESUS I Knew

The JESUS *I Knew*

Creative Portrayals of Gospel Characters

ROBERT MARTIN WALKER

ABINGDON PRESS
Nashville

THE JESUS I KNEW
CREATIVE PORTRAYALS OF GOSPEL CHARACTERS

Copyright © 1996 by Abingdon Press

All rights reserved.
No part of this work may be reproduced or transmitted in any form or by any means, electronic or mechanical, including photocopying and recording, or by any information storage or retrieval system, except as may be expressly permitted by the 1976 Copyright Act or in writing from the publisher. Requests for permission should be addressed in writing to Abingdon Press, 201 Eighth Avenue South, Nashville, TN 37203.

This book is printed on acid-free, recycled paper.

Scripture quotations, unless otherwise noted, are from the New Revised Standard Version of the Bible, copyright © 1989 by the Division of Christian Education of the National Council of the Churches of Christ in the USA.

Library of Congress Cataloging-in-Publication Data

Walker, Robert Martin.
    The Jesus I knew : creative portrayals of Gospel characters / Robert Martin Walker.
      p.   cm.
    ISBN 0-687-10931-0 (alk. paper)
    1. Bible. N.T. Gospels—Biography. 2. Bible. N.T. Gospels—Devotional literature. I. Title.
BS2555.4.W35 1996
226'.0922—cc20   96-17508
                                                      CIP

00 01 02 03 04 05 — 10 9 8 7 6 5 4

MANUFACTURED IN THE UNITED STATES OF AMERICA

*With deepest love and gratitude
to my parents, Bob and Eileen,
whose Christian faith nurtures and
inspires me to this day*

Acknowledgments

There are so many persons to thank for their role in the conception and writing of this book that an entire chapter would be needed to name them all. I gratefully mention the communities that have helped shape my understanding of the gospel: the faculties of Perkins School of Theology/SMU and Yale University Divinity School; the congregations of Central United Methodist Church in Albuquerque; Chisholm United Methodist Church, Oak Lawn United Methodist Church, and Richland United Methodist Church in Texas; and Darien United Methodist Church in Connecticut.

I am also grateful to the New York Annual Conference and its former bishop, Forrest Stith, for allowing me a one-year sabbatical in 1993-94, during which I wrote *The Jesus I Knew*.

And with deep appreciation I thank my wife, Donna, who has served as editor, confidante, and companion on the Journey. Without her unflagging and enthusiastic support, this book would not have been written.

Cast of Characters

Act IV: Jesus' Resurrection

Introduction
Setting the Stage

What would it be like to hear Mary's reaction to the news that she would be the mother of God's Son? If we could hear from Judas, how would he justify his betrayal of Jesus? If Peter could speak to us, how would he explain his denial of the Lord? How would Lazarus describe being brought from death to life? What words would Mary Magdalene use to tell of her encounter with the Risen Lord on Easter?

The writers of the Gospels weren't interested in answering these questions, even if they could. Rather, they focused on the actions and words of Jesus. Yet, as a preacher and teacher, I have often wondered about the thoughts and feelings of the men and women in the Gospel drama. I don't believe I'm alone in my curiosity.

This book is a journey into uncharted territory. Using interpretation and imagination, it is a collection of twenty-five portraits of characters in the Gospels. In creating these portraits I have attempted to be faithful to the scripture texts on which they are based, and also to capture the unique voice of each character. The mixture of imagination and interpretation varies from character to character. Where the Bible is silent, imagination fills in the spaces. Where the Bible speaks, I have carefully followed the text. The result is imagination that is disciplined by the Word.

My process for writing a portrait has been to start with the biblical text and then imagine how the character would narrate a story from his or her own point of view. In respecting the unique witness of each Gospel, I have stayed within a single Gospel for each portrayal, with a few exceptions. For example, while Matthew's portrayal of Peter is similar to John's, there are differences that must be honored.

By creatively combining two methods of storytelling, narrative and autobiography, these portraits have the power to draw you, the reader, inside the Gospel story. I hope that by seeing Jesus through the eyes of the characters who knew him best, you will hear the gospel message in a new and fresh way. These portraits can be springboards for using your own imagination in reading the scriptures.

If the gospel story seems dull and unengaging, it is because we have not been willing to enter into the world it creates. The problem is not with the scriptures, but with our lack of imagination in reading them.

The characters of the Bible were living, thinking, feeling human beings, like you and me. They had emotions and passions, loves and hates, dreams and disappointments. To see them as the real persons they were can encourage us to identify with them and to share their faith in the One whom they knew as Lord and Savior.

What finally emerges from these testimonies is a portrait of who Jesus was, and is. These characters offer their distinctive witnesses to the birth, ministry, passion, and resurrection of our Lord. In hearing their testimonies, our own faith can be enriched and enlivened.

Many of you will use *The Jesus I Knew* in a time of personal devotions to deepen your spiritual life. The book also lends itself to group settings: group devotions, Sunday school classes, Bible study groups, drama, and preaching. I have included three or more questions with each portrait that could be used as discussion starters. Several of these portraits had their birth in sermons I have preached. Nothing would please me more than to know that these characters are giving their "testimonies" in worship services.

As you enter into the lives of these Gospel characters, I hope that their stories of Jesus will inspire and strengthen your own faith. May the Jesus they knew as Lord and Savior lead you to a deeper knowledge of and faith in Jesus Christ.

Robert Martin Walker

Act I
Jesus' Birth

Mary, Mother of Jesus

Read Luke 1:26-38.

"Greetings, favored one! The Lord is with you." (v. 28)

What is this vision that startles me awake? The voice comes from a creature of light. It sounds calm and soothing like the gentle flowing of a river or the rising and falling of the tide. I am almost lulled back to sleep by the angel's voice, but then questions start flooding my mind.

Why is this vision coming to me? How am I to be favored? What is the meaning of this greeting?

I am confused and afraid. The angel says that the Lord is with me. That should be enough to calm my fears, but I am still anxious.

"Do not be afraid, Mary, for you have found favor with God." (v. 30)

I am trying to be brave, to be open to the words of light. The angel says I have God's favor and that is good, isn't it? My sisters in the faith also had God's favor: Sarah, Ruth, and Naomi. But they had such difficult lives. Sarah was childless until she was old, having to bear the humiliation of barrenness while Abraham had a son with Hagar. Ruth finally found love, but only after losing her husband to death and working in the fields. And Naomi knew the triple pain of losing a husband and two sons. Do I *really* want God's favor? Am I strong enough to bear it?

"And now, you will conceive in your womb and bear a son."
(v. 31a)

How can this be? I am not fully married; my time of betrothal isn't yet over. I am still living at my parents' home until I am of age. Surely, the angel means that I will have Joseph's child. What else could this mean? Surely the angel didn't say *now*. To become pregnant before I go to live with Joseph at his parents' home would be a disaster! Yes, the angel must be talking about some time in the distant future.

"You will name him Jesus. He will be great, and will be called the Son of the Most High." (vv. 31b, 32)

The angel says the child will be God's son. I don't know what this means, but I know that the name Jesus means "God will save." I am pleased that my son will be great. What mother wouldn't want greatness in a son? Perhaps he will be a king, a ruler of men. I feel pride welling up within me. But what does it mean that he will be "Son of the Most High"?

"The Holy Spirit will come upon you, and the power of the Most High will overshadow you." (v. 35a)

The angel's words are so reassuring, so calming. They are almost enough to overcome my fears. I envision the peace of the Lord washing over me like warm waters, cleansing the fear from my soul. I feel enveloped in safety. I feel protected.

"Therefore the child to be born will be holy; he will be called Son of God." (v. 35b)

I am perplexed again. How can this child be Joseph's son and God's son at the same time? As I ponder this, I feel a stab of fear. It feels like a knife piercing my heart as it dawns upon me: *This child will not be Joseph's!*

The angel told me to not be afraid, but I am terrified! I visualize myself growing larger each day. What will happen when I can't hide my condition? In my mind I already see Mother staring at my belly a second too long.

What am I going to do? I cannot run away. I have no means of support. I have no place to hide. I have no husband.

Who is this child that will grow within me? What does it mean that he will be called "Son of God"? What will others think of me once they discover I'm pregnant?

And what will Joseph think of me? I hardly know him. I want us to learn to love each other, but how can our young love bear such a crushing weight? Just like everyone else, he will think I am an adulteress. My parents will cast me out. I will be raising this child alone, working in fields where I am not known, just like Naomi did. How could this be happening to me? Is this God's *favor*?

I can picture it when I walk out of Nazareth. The women and children will line the streets, turning their backs to me as I walk by. They will make clicking noises with their tongues, the sounds of scorn.

But I am thinking too much about myself and not enough about the child. What will become of him if he is raised without a father? He will have a hard life, working the fields with me from the time he is old enough to walk.

How can I be a good mother to him? And what will happen when he learns he has no father? Will he love me enough to forgive me? Will he believe the unbelievable story of an angelic vision?

This all seems so . . . impossible. How can this birth happen?

"For nothing will be impossible with God." (v. 37)

I feel a sense of assurance returning. My hands are no longer shaking. Yes, it will be difficult birthing and raising this promised child. But I will do it, even if I am alone and in a strange place.

I will place my trust in the Lord no matter what happens. The Lord who created me and surrounded me with steadfast love will not desert me in my time of need. "The Lord is with you," the angel said. That must be enough for me when I bear this child, God's child. I will accept whatever God wants to do with me. I will serve the Lord with all that I am and all that I have.

Unbelievably, I hear myself saying aloud, "Here I am, the servant of the Lord; let it be with me according to your word."

Dear Lord, give me the faith of Mary who, though perplexed, accepted God's impossible news. When I am anxious or afraid, may I know what Mary knew: that the Lord is with me. Let me be open to however the Lord wants to use me. Amen.

For Reflection and Discussion

- What would be your initial reaction if you had received Mary's news? What emotions would you feel?
- When have you been asked to believe a promise that seemed impossible? What happened?
- What allowed Mary to accept God's word and submit to it? What enables you to do the same?

Joseph, Husband of Mary

Read Matthew 1:18-25.

"Joseph, son of David, do not be afraid to take Mary as your wife."
(v. 20b)

I must be dreaming again. Lately, it is happening more and more. I seem to be following in the footsteps of my ancestor, Joseph the son of Jacob, for whom I am named.

I am asleep and then, without warning, the angel appears. Until now, this figure in blazing white has not spoken. But now I am addressed.

What the angel asks of me I cannot do. A year ago, I would not have said this. A year ago, as we stood before the Rabbi and our families reciting the vows of marriage, the thought of taking Mary as my wife was as intoxicating as new wine. But now . . .

Now she is *pregnant*, and not by me! I don't know who the father is, and I don't care. The truth is: *I care very much*. When she told me the news, I was so deeply hurt I wanted to lash back at her in vengeance. I wanted her to suffer as much as I did. The Torah says that I could have pressed charges against Mary and humiliated her publicly. For a time, I contemplated such revenge.

Then, as days became weeks, my heart softened toward her. She shouldn't be condemned for one mistake, I told myself. So I decided to divorce her quietly, without any furor. Since we have not yet started living together, the divorce would not be too harmful to her. Yes, she would be viewed as immoral, but that is hardly my fault. At least she would escape the label "adulteress."

Many times I have gathered my courage and walked toward her family's home to tell her of my decision. But something always holds me back. I realize that I don't want to divorce her, that I want to keep her as my wife, even though I would be the one humiliated.

Still, I cannot condone what she has done. I can forgive her but I cannot stop hurting, knowing that someone has loved her before me. My pain is like an open wound, oozing bitterness.

I am afraid to take her as my wife. I am afraid of what my father, Jacob, will say, when my young bride's belly begins to thicken too soon after we begin living together. I am afraid of what our friends will think of us. Most of all, I am afraid of how I might treat Mary. Can I ever forgive this injury to my soul? Will it fester until I cannot love her again? Will I end up losing my respect for her and treat her with contempt? Yes, I am afraid.

"For the child conceived in her is from the Holy Spirit." (v. 20c)

I don't understand. What does the angel mean? Whose child is Mary carrying? How can a child be conceived of God's Spirit? Could the angel be telling me that Mary's child is *God's* Child?

No, that is more than impossible; it is too incredible to be believed. Never before has a child been conceived from the Spirit of God. Surely, I'm not expected to believe such an unthinkable story.

But I want to believe it. If it were true, it would explain so much. When I demanded to know of Mary who the father was, she was silent. When I angrily pressed her for an answer, she quietly said, "You wouldn't believe me if I told you." I thought that she was covering for her lover, even though she had not given me reason to doubt her word. Until then, Mary had not lied to me.

It would also explain why there was no guilt in Mary's eyes when I accused her of unfaithfulness. Her eyes shone with a sad innocence at my charges, which made me even more enraged. Could she truly be innocent, as the angel says?

If only it could be true that Mary is innocent. I still love her. No matter what she has done, I love her with all my heart.

"She will bear a son, and you are to name him Jesus." (v. 21a)

This dream is too much for me. I am overwhelmed, awestruck, and dumbfounded. Not only is this child God's Son, I am to accept him as my own son! Only a father can give a son his true name. In naming this child of Mary's, I claim him as my own.

My fears are returning. If this child is God's child, how can I be his father? I am human. And God . . . well, God is God. The creature cannot be above the Creator. I am only a humble carpenter, barely scraping out a living. Never, even in my dreams, could I imagine raising God's Son.

But the child will need a father. Even God's child will need to be fed and cared for. And if I do not take Mary as my wife, this child will be doomed to a life of mockery and humiliation. I could save him from such a horrible fate. Every child needs a father.

Deep down I know that being a father has little to do with the moment of conception. Fathering is raising a son with love and care. Fathering is teaching a son the Torah and setting an example of obedience. Fathering is training a child in the way he should grow.

Just as this child is growing within Mary, the idea of being a father is growing in me. Yes, I will obey the angel's command, because it is from God.

I will name this child Jesus.

Jesus. Already I am growing used to the name. It conveys power and humility, gentleness and authority.

From my studies of the Torah I know that *Jesus* comes from the ancient name *Joshua*. If Jesus is anything like his ancestor Joshua, I will be proud. Joshua was a leader and commander of men. He led our nation into the promised land of Canaan and presided over its conquest. Joshua was courageous and righteous.

"For he will save his people from their sins." (v. 21b)

The name *Jesus* means "God will save." But I am confused again. How will Jesus save us from our sins? Will he cast out the Romans and reestablish Jewish rule in Israel? Will he become a great rabbi and give us new interpretations of the Torah? Will he become the high priest and offer sacrifices in the temple?

Although I do not understand how Jesus will save us, I find myself believing the words of the angel. I will follow the angel's command and take Mary as my wife and claim this child—God's child—as my son. I will do this because God commands it. And I will do it willingly because I love Mary.

Dear Lord, give me the obedience of Joseph. When I am hurt, give me the strength to forgive. When I don't understand, help me to trust. When I am afraid, may your love overcome my fears. In the name of Jesus, I pray. Amen.

For Reflection and Discussion

- If you had received Joseph's dream, how would you have reacted?
- What enables you to forgive when you have been hurt? How is it possible to love someone you believe has betrayed you?
- What qualities of character does Joseph demonstrate? Which of these would you like to possess?

Elizabeth, Mother of John

Read Luke 1:5-25, 39-80.

When Zechariah came home from the temple unable to speak, I was terrified. He was staring wide-eyed and waving his arms wildly as though possessed by a demon. He looked as frightened as I felt.

He kept gesturing frantically, and with growing frustration, because I had no idea what he was trying to tell me. Finally, he collapsed at my feet and cried a pool of tears.

"Please, Zechariah, calm down. You'll be all right." I tried to sound more confident than I felt. I bent down and wrapped my arms around him as if he was the baby I never had, but he was inconsolable. Suddenly, I thought of a way he could tell me what happened.

"Stay there, Zech, I'll be back in a minute." I left him sitting on the floor and ran into the kitchen. On a shelf above the pots I found the writing tablet. I rushed the tablet and a stylus to him.

When he realized what I had brought, he leaped to his feet with the excitement of a child. His hands were shaking so badly, I could barely read the words he scribbled. I made out the words *angel* and *baby* and *John*. When he stopped writing, I was still baffled. What was he trying to tell me? I nodded my head as if I understood, hoping to pacify him. Realizing I didn't understand, he became even more agitated, ramming his finger against the tablet several times.

"Please, Zech, write slowly and start at the beginning. I want to understand." When he finished writing—clearly this time—I was terrified that Zech had lost his mind. He wrote that we were going to have a baby!

A baby! The thought of being a mother was beyond my wildest dreams. All of my adult life I had endured the curse of barrenness. When I was younger, my mother and sisters would ask the question that eventually was torture for me to hear, "When are you and Zechariah going to be parents?" After years had passed and there was no baby, they stopped asking. But I never stopped hoping and longing for a child.

When my monthly bleeding stopped, my last hope to be a mother dried up. I had to accept the fact that Zechariah and I would have no offspring. I was doomed to a life of childlessness, a life of disgrace.

I wanted to believe Zechariah the day he came home from the temple without a voice. I ached that the news he wrote on the tablet would come true. I dreamed of reliving the story of my ancestor Sarah, who had Isaac when she was past childbearing years. Only a miracle could make me pregnant.

Months passed when—joy of joys—my dream for a child actually came true! My waist had grown thick; my body proclaimed what my mind still couldn't believe. *I was pregnant!* Like Sarah, I laughed at the sheer marvel of the news. Zechariah, who still couldn't speak, cried tears of joy and relief.

I wanted to run down the streets of our village shouting the news, "I am going to be a mother!" But I quickly reconsidered. What if something went wrong? What if I lost this child of promise? So I stayed at home with Zechariah, savoring this joyous secret in private.

When I was in my sixth month, I had a surprise visitor. Mary, a distant relative from Nazareth, came for a visit. I was delighted when she walked through the door. Mary had always been one of my favorites, even though she was so many years younger.

At her greeting, I felt a strange sensation in my womb. The baby felt as if it was leaping out of me. Could my unborn child have recognized Mary's voice? Suddenly, I understood! I looked at Mary and cried out with words that were not my own.

"Blessed are you among women, and blessed is the fruit of your womb. And why has this happened to me, that the mother of my Lord comes to me?" (vv. 42-43).

I explained to Mary how my child had leaped for joy at the sound of her voice. Mary said that she already knew I was pregnant and told me that she was also carrying a child. We embraced in gladness.

I added another blessing, "Blessed is she who believed that there would be a fulfillment of what was spoken to her by the Lord" (v. 45).

Mary, filled with ecstasy, then sang the most beautiful hymn I had ever heard. She sang of the greatness of the Lord and of her own lowliness. She sang of how the lowly would be exalted and the powerful humbled. She ended by praising God for remembering Israel and the promises he made to us. When Mary finished, I was awestruck.

For three months, Mary stayed with me and we enjoyed each other's company. Zechariah was pleased that Mary shared our home. Her presence made our solitude less lonely. When she returned to Galilee, she was beginning to show.

Our child, a boy, was born a few days after Mary left. I was attended by several relatives, who couldn't stop talking about how miraculous this joyful event was.

On the eighth day, it was time to circumcise our son. My relatives wanted to name him Zechariah, which would have been proper according to tradition.

But I said, "No, he will be called John."

They objected, saying that none of our ancestors had that name. An argument broke out. Finally, my brother-in-law,

Micah, shouted, "Let's ask Zechariah what the name shall be."

Zechariah wrote on the tablet and Micah read the words to everyone, "His name is John." The room was filled with open mouths and raised eyebrows.

Suddenly, a man's voice began praising God. It was Zechariah. His tongue had been freed! My relatives and neighbors shied away from him, not knowing what to think about this outburst. Some ran out the door. I overheard someone whisper, "What then will this child become?" (v. 66).

My husband's voice became louder and clearer. He launched into a prophecy that filled the room. He spoke of a coming Savior from the house of David. He proclaimed the Lord's mighty acts of old and his promise to Abraham. Then, to my amazement, he spoke of our child, John.

"And you, child, will be called the prophet of the Most High; for you will go before the Lord to prepare his ways" (v. 76).

My heart leaped at the thought that our son would play a part in God's redemption of Israel. He will be a *prophet!* He will prepare the way for the coming Savior! I felt twice blessed. Not only had I been given a son, but he would serve the Lord in a special way. What mother could ask for more?

My attention was torn away from my husband by our son's cries. I cradled little John in my arms, comforting him after the pain of circumcision. "You will be a great prophet," I whispered to him. "You are indeed a child of joy."

Almighty God, who speaks through prophets and poets, I give you thanks for your Word spoken through different people. Help me trust your Word always, even when it seems unbelievable. May I never stop believing that your promises will be fulfilled. In Jesus' name I pray. Amen.

For Reflection and Discussion

- How are the stories of Sarah/Abraham and Eliza-beth/Zechariah similar? How do they differ? (See Genesis 18:1-15; 21:1-7.)
- When have you endured "barrenness" (literally or figuratively)? How did you feel? How did you respond?
- When have you known the kind of overwhelming joy of Elizabeth when she meets Mary? What was the source of that joy?
- In what ways does the story of your life intersect the story of Elizabeth? In what ways can you take part in preparing the way of the Lord?

The Shepherd Boy

Read Luke 2:8-20.

One clear winter night I was helping my father and brothers herd our small flock into the sheepfold. As the youngest, I always had to run after the strays who were trying to eat one last mouthful of grass. The night was cold, and it was way past my bedtime.

Being a shepherd is really hard work. You can never leave a flock alone. Sheep are pretty stupid. That makes them an easy dinner for wolves and robbers. A shepherd must always be alert. Danger is everywhere.

I went to bed as soon as all the sheep had been counted. I was glad that I had several hours before it was my turn to watch. I curled into a tight ball in my scratchy wool blanket, trying to keep warm, and slept.

The next thing I knew I was awakened by some noises. It must have been deep into the night because the stars shone like thousands of tiny campfires. I heard the voices of my father and uncle outside the hut where my brothers, cousins, and I slept. They sounded very excited and afraid, like they had just run off a pack of wolves. I listened carefully and thought I heard singing. It wasn't like any music I had ever heard.

Suddenly, my father and uncle came running into our hut yelling, "Boys! Wake up! We are going to Bethlehem!"

My first thought was that my father had drunk too much wine. Sometimes during the long and lonely nights with nobody to talk to except the sheep, his wineskin would keep him company. I got close to him to smell his breath, but there was no wine odor. My brothers and cousins who had got less sleep than I had were grumbling about leaving the warm cocoons of their beds on a chilly night.

My uncle shouted excitedly, "Boys! Get up! Quickly! We have a long way to travel! The Savior has been born!"

After hearing this I was sure that my father and uncle had been enjoying too much wine. I wondered why I couldn't smell it on their breaths.

"What do you mean, Father?" I asked. "You want us to go there *now*, in the middle of the night?"

He motioned for us to gather round him, and he spoke in an awed whisper. "Hosea and I have seen a vision of angels. We were keeping watch over the flock and the heavens opened and it was as bright as noon. Then we saw an angel! We cowered in fear. But the angel said to us, 'Do not be afraid. I am bringing you good news of great joy. Today, in the city of David, a Savior has been born who is the Messiah. This will be a sign that I am speaking truly: you will find a baby wrapped in bands of cloth lying in a manger.' Then, other angels appeared, countless in number, singing praises to God!"

Uncle Hosea looked strange. His eyes were focused trance-like on the far horizon. He shook his head up and down saying, "Yes, yes. We must go to Bethlehem!"

My brothers, cousins, and I couldn't believe how weird our fathers were acting. But we were too stunned to ask any more questions. For the first time ever we left the sheep alone. I worried about whether they would be alive when we returned. Quickly I petted Balaam, my favorite, and told him to be careful.

The twelve-mile journey to Bethlehem passed quickly. My father and uncle practically ran the whole way. It was all my brothers, cousins, and I could do to keep up with them. Strangely, I don't remember feeling cold, even though I could see my breath. Nor do I remember anyone saying anything during our journey. A single thought kept repeating in my mind: Tomorrow these two drunken shepherds will be sorry they made us leave the sheep alone.

On the way to Bethlehem I thought about what my father claimed he saw. I kept asking myself *Why?* Why would angels of the Lord bother with lowly shepherds? We weren't wealthy. We weren't powerful. There weren't many jobs worse than shepherding. We were treated like outcasts by almost everyone. Because we couldn't leave the sheep alone, we weren't able to attend the religious festivals or make regular offerings at the temple. The priests called us "unclean" and looked down on us for not following all their silly rules. My brothers and I couldn't attend the temple school. Sheep couldn't be left alone—except for tonight.

It was still dark when we got to Bethlehem. My heart sank as I saw the thousands of families encamped there for the census. I had heard about the Emperor's order that everyone was to be counted. That probably meant new taxes. The Romans never lowered taxes. Shepherds generally ignored these decrees. Our moving around in the countryside made it impossible for tax collectors to find us.

My father began asking anyone we met, "Do you know where the Savior has been born?" One man said something crude while another laughed like my father had made a hilarious joke. I was beginning to question my father's sanity. He had had plenty of time to sober up.

Then my uncle said to Father, "Malachi. Remember the words of the angel. We will find the Savior in a manger." I wondered if my uncle knew how many stables there were in Bethlehem.

My father said, "Yes! How could I have forgotten! Let's search for a stable."

My brother John objected, "But there must be many stables in Bethlehem, and it is still night. How can we find the right one?"

Even though I knew it was crazy, we split into two groups and began to search for a stable with a baby in it. We agreed to meet at the first light of dawn at the inn we had passed coming into town. My father, brothers, and I wandered through the streets of Bethlehem like blind men. We listened for the noises of animals in the still of the night. These sounds would lead us to the stables. After hours of hunting we had found seven stables but no Savior.

Just before dawn we found my uncle and cousins waiting for us in front of the inn. They also had found several stables but none with a baby. I could tell by the look on my father's face that he was beginning to question the angel's words—if there ever was an angel. By now I was really worried about the sheep we had left alone. I wanted to go home.

Just as I was about to say that we should return home, I heard a weak moan. "Quiet! Do you hear that?" I asked. In the silence, the noise became clearer. It was the gentle lowing of a cow coming from behind the inn. We ran around to the back of the inn and found a stable. To my everlasting surprise, a family was in the stable among the animals! And there in a manger was a *baby!* The cow was lowing because the baby lay on top of the straw she wanted to eat.

My father humbly approached the family in the stable like they were royalty. He told the mother and father about the vision of angels and how he was told he would find a baby—a Savior—wrapped in cloths and lying in a manger.

The parents looked surprised by my father's story, but not as much as I expected. Mainly they seemed tired. They said nothing; but the young mother smiled wearily, slightly turning up the edges of her mouth. She looked like she was thinking about my father's story. While she thought, I craned my neck to catch a glimpse of the baby the angel said was the Messiah. He looked like a newborn lamb—red and wrinkled. He didn't look any different than any other baby. I don't know what I expected.

We stayed just a few minutes. There seemed to be nothing more to say. We returned home as quickly as we had come. Even though we had barely slept, the journey home was somehow easier and our steps lighter. Joy was with us.

The sun rose higher over the horizon. The beginning of a new day. To greet the morning my father and uncle began to sing a song of praise to God they had learned as boys. My brothers and cousins joined in singing the familiar tune. Finally I added my voice to the notes of praise and glory. What else could we do, knowing that the Savior had been born?

Dear Lord, who gave the world a Savior, give my heart wings to fly to Bethlehem and see the Christ Child. Open my eyes to Christ's presence in daily life. Open my ears to hear the music of angels. Open my heart to receive him. In the name of the Christ Child I pray. Amen.

For Reflection and Discussion

- Why do you think the shepherds were first to hear the news of Christ's birth? How has humility made you more receptive to God?
- When has your initial skepticism given way to faith?
- Where do you hear the singing of angels and experience the joy of the Christ Child in your life?
- In what ways have you taken the journey of the shepherds in your own life?

Anna the Prophetess

Read Luke 2:25-38.

I am praying when the words of Simeon drift into my ears as if carried by the wind. The urgency of the words stop my prayers. I listen carefully but can't make them out. My hearing is fading like the rest of me.

The grass withers, the flower fades, but the Word of the Lord endures forever.

What I can hear is the tenor of his voice. I hear excitement-wonder, awe-joy. The words lift me off my aching knees as if they have a power of their own.

In the distance I can make out three hazy figures. My eyesight is not so good anymore, either. I stumble toward them as if drunk. I can't walk as steadily as I used to, but I am being drawn by the words. Now the forms are clearer. Simeon is at the altar with a man and a woman. He is holding something in his arms, but I need to get closer to make it out.

Now I am close enough to see and hear. Simeon's face is glowing with joy, and he is holding a *baby!* I tilt my better ear toward him. He looks at the woman and says,

"This child is destined for the falling and the rising of many in Israel, and to be a sign that will be opposed so that the inner thoughts of many will be revealed—and a sword will pierce your own soul too." (vv. 34-35)

I stop walking and clutch at my heart to calm its drumming. *Simeon is prophesying about the Messiah!* How many years have I been in this temple, hoping, longing, waiting to see the Redeemer? I think it has been eighty-four, but my memory is fading too since Hasshub died. We had only seven years together, and the memory of him is so distant that I can no longer imagine his face. Now these stone walls are my only home. Here I fast and pray and wait. I could have remarried, but I chose to be God's bride instead.

As I squint to see the child more clearly, I am struck with a knowing that comes from beyond sense and sight and sound. *This child is the Messiah!* I feel tears wet my wrinkled-dried cheeks as Simeon holds the child high above him like a priest offering a sacrifice. He spoke of a sword piercing the mother's soul, and I feel my own heart rent by this Child.

How can this be happening to me? I am old and forgotten, having outlived even the memories of my life. I am of the tribe of Asher, the least of the Twelve. I am a widow, dependent on the generosity of names I cannot remember. I am the least of God's servants, even though some call me a prophetess. But the Child drives these thoughts away like a healer exorcising demons.

As I behold the Child, there is only praise and wonder that the Lord would allow me to see him before my death, which can't be far away. I open my mouth to speak, and words of praise beyond my eloquence are released. I am a pouring pitcher, a gushing well. The praises flow through me and echo in the temple's silence. A song is woven from the word-notes, and the music is beautiful. I am swaying with the melody like a timbrel dancer, and a crowd has gathered. I sing:

This is the Messiah, the Long-Awaited One. The Lord has given him to us for Judgment and Redemption, Consolation and Salvation. Praise the Lord for his great mercy and everlasting love!

I sing until the praises have dried up. I have spent my life-energy playing this music as God's instrument of praise. I feel myself falling, falling. Before I float down to the stone-cold floor and close my eyes in long-desired sleep, I catch a final glimpse of the Messiah, and that is enough to sustain my eternal dream.

The grass withers, the flower fades, but the Word of the Lord endures forever.

Dear Lord, help me to wait faithfully like Anna, who worshiped you continually. Open my ears to modern-day prophets who proclaim the presence of Jesus Christ in our midst. Open my eyes that I, too, may glimpse your Son in daily life. In Jesus' name I pray. Amen.

For Reflection and Discussion

• What is important enough to you that you would wait many years for it? What does it mean to wait faithfully?
• How do Simeon and Anna testify to the Messiah's coming? In what ways do you testify to Jesus' daily presence?
• What words of praise do you imagine Anna used to proclaim the Messiah's coming? What words do you use to praise God?

Herod the Great

Read Matthew 2:1-18.

I was exceedingly curious about the three strangers dressed in royal robes who entered my chambers. For days there had been rumors of holy men traveling from the East to Jerusalem. It was said that they were seeking a king. I was anxious to see their reaction upon finding one.

My curiosity quickly changed to astonishment. Rather than paying me, Herod the Great, homage, they asked, "Where is the child who has been born king of the Jews?"

I looked down on them from my throne incredulously. Here were three strangers, dressed in the robes of scholars, standing before the King of the Jews asking where he may be found. *"I am King of the Jews!"* I wanted to scream. Did these strangers know with whom they were dealing? Did they have even a hint of the vast power of the one they were offending? I held the power of life and death in this corner of the world. One word from me and they would be destroyed!

They could not know the lengths to which I was willing to go to protect my kingship. Over the years, I had murdered my rivals, slaughtered my enemies in battle, and had my first wife slain for adultery. I had survived the Great Civil War, having fought for Cassius, the victor. My crown was won by blood and treachery; I would never give it up. Instead of divulging my thoughts, I held my tongue. Experience had taught me to wait for opponents to reveal their weaknesses.

Then the tallest stranger spoke. He talked of a star they had been following and how it had led them to Judea. They asked me for the exact location of the king's birth, assuming that I would know it. I sent them away, telling them I would consult my advisers and give them an answer the next day. Strangely, the mention of the star sent a chill down my back. The guiding star was said to be a sign of the Messiah's coming. Over the years, I had heard speculations about a so-called Messiah who would save the Jews from Roman rule. I passed this off as the crazy talk of idlers. Every time a foreign ruler oppressed our nation, rabbis started preaching about a coming Savior.

After they left I dismissed my advisers, threw myself onto the floor, and pounded my fists on the cold marble until blood ran freely. I screamed to the attendants standing outside the door to summon the Sanhedrin at once. Perhaps the pompous Jews who made up the Council of Seventy-One could tell me where this so-called king known as the Messiah was supposed to be born. They had better be able to tell me. The Sanhedrin existed at my pleasure. Once, it had genuine power and ruled the Jews in all matters, civil and religious. However, I declawed the Council and restricted its authority to meaningless religious issues. I remember the surprise of Hyrcanus, who was the high priest at the time. He was shocked that I, a Jew by birth, would tamper with "God's Tribunal," as he called the Sanhedrin. For opposing my plan, Hyrcanus paid with his life, condemned by the very council he sought to protect. From then on, I appointed the high priest and, therefore, controlled the Sanhedrin.

The Sanhedrin convened and discussed the mission of the holy men from the East. They soon gave me the answer I sought. The Messiah was to be born in Bethlehem. Once I had what I wanted, I dismissed the priest and scribes. Then, I had my most trusted adviser, Syranius, arrange a secret meeting with the holy men.

When they came to my chambers a second time, I offered these emissaries from the East an exchange of information. I would tell them where the king they sought was prophesied to be born if they would tell me when the guiding star first appeared. These fools were only too glad to tell me what I wanted to know. Seeing their gullibility, I sent them to Bethlehem to find this so-called king and asked them to return to me with word of the child's exact location so that I might worship him also. To my amazement they took me at my word. Yes, I *would* worship this pretender king—with the sharp edge of a sword!

After they left I was elated at how easily I manipulated these holy fools. They would do the searching for me. And, once they returned from Bethlehem, I would make certain this child was no longer a threat.

I waited one week. Then two. After a month, I panicked. I sent spies to Bethlehem to learn what had happened to the holy men. They returned with frightening news: the holy men had left for their eastern home only a few days after arriving in Bethlehem.

I had been tricked! I, who prided myself on treachery, had been double-crossed! Enraged, I summoned my advisers and asked them what should be done about this child-king whose very existence threatened my hold on Judea. They came up with various plans to find the child, none of which had any guarantees because they didn't know the age of the child.

I revealed to them that I knew the approximate age of the child because of the time of the star's appearing, and I told them of my plan. I ordered my commanders to kill all male children under two years of age in Bethlehem and the surrounding villages. Even though the child would not yet be one year of age, according to the time the holy men saw the star, I wanted to be certain. The holy fools would pay for their deceit. The blood of many children would be on *their* heads.

The expressions of horror and revulsion on the faces of my advisers amused me. They were soft of head and heart, unwilling to wield the necessary force to maintain power. That is why I am king and they are not. A king's reign lasts only as long as his subjects' fear.

A week later, my chief commander brought word that my order had been carried out. I was relieved to hear it. No mere child would threaten the power of Herod the Great! Messiah, indeed! Any messiah who could be so easily killed wasn't really a king in the first place.

Almighty God, who sent your Son into the world to save me, with the eyes of faith may I see your guiding star and follow it. Allow it to lead me to the Savior, where I may worship and honor him as King. In the name of Jesus, I pray. Amen.

For Reflection and Discussion

- What kind of king is Herod? Why is he threatened by news of the Messiah's birth?
- When have you been afraid to give up power over someone or something? If you gave up that power, what happened?
- What is the "guiding star" that you are following in your journey of faith? What gifts are you willing to offer Christ?

Act II
Jesus' Ministry

John the Baptizer

Read Matthew 3:1-17; 11:2-15; 14:1-12.

The days drag on like years. The nights seem even longer, if that is possible. No light reaches down here. I have lost track of how many weeks have passed. Day or night makes no difference in Herod's dungeon.

Here there is only waiting. I wait for the one meager meal I am served each day. I wait for the frequent beatings by cruel guards. I wait for the weekly visit from my disciples. I wait to hear news of whether I will live or die.

I am good at waiting because it is my vocation. All of my life I have been waiting for the Messiah. Six months ago I thought I had found him.

A few hours before he came to me, I was preaching, exhorting the large crowd gathered on the banks of the Jordan to repent of their sin and be baptized. Because I offer a baptism of repentance, I am called, "John the Baptizer."

My message that day, and every day, was the same. "Repent! God's Messiah is coming and you'd better be ready. The Lord despises sin and will punish every iniquity. Only God's everlasting mercy holds back the fires of wrath from raining down on us as they did on Sodom and Gomorrah," I warned.

"When the Messiah comes, the words of the prophet will be fulfilled: 'Justice will roll down like waters and righteousness like everflowing streams,'" I preached.

I believed with all my heart that the time of the Messiah's coming was near. I yearned for the day when the Lord would send the Coming One to set things right by punishing sinners and rewarding the righteous.

Why do I believe that the Messiah is coming? Because our world is in a horrendous mess. The pagan Romans rule over us as if we were stupid sheep. They erect blasphemous idols of stone outside the temple and worship them. Their drunken orgies, cruelty, and public immorality are all offensive to God.

That's not the worst of it. Our leaders *tolerate* these abominations. Weak and afraid, they refuse to battle the evils inflicted upon us by Rome. We are decaying like rotted fruit.

Of our leaders, the most despicable hypocrites are the Pharisees and Sadducees. They came to me that day in the morning. When I saw them walking down the river bank with their expensive robes and servants, I wanted to vomit.

"You brood of vipers! Who warned you to flee from the coming wrath of God?" I shouted at them. "If you truly want to repent, then start living according to God's will." I could *smell* the insincerity seeping from their pores, and the stench sickened me.

They drew nearer despite my railings. When I saw the smug, self-satisfied expressions on their faces, I exploded.

"You think you're going to be spared from God's wrath because you are Abraham's children? That counts for *nothing* in the Kingdom of God! Even now God is wielding an ax and will cut at the root of every tree that does not bear fruit *and burn it!*"

I sent them away with a final blast. "The Messiah is coming, and he will not baptize with water as I do. He will baptize with the Holy Spirit and with fire. He is coming with a winnowing fork to separate the wheat from the chaff. The wheat will be gathered into the storehouse, but the chaff he will burn with unquenchable fire!"

I could see rage burning in the eyes of those snakes before they slithered away. I was glad to see them go.

That happened in the morning.

At high noon, a man I had never seen before walked toward me as if he knew me. With each step he took, an awareness grew within me. My spirit soared when I realized I was seeing the Coming One!

How did I know he was the Messiah? I cannot explain, but I believed it with all my heart on that day.

He waded into the Jordan and stopped in front of me. He motioned for me to baptize him. I was stunned. "Why does the Messiah need to be baptized by me?" I wondered.

I said to the stranger, "I should be baptized by you, not you by me."

He said, "Let it be this way for now. In this way we will fulfill the will of God."

Although I didn't understand it, I baptized this man who gave his name as Jesus. "He has a messianic name," I thought. "*Jesus* means 'God will save.'"

I dunked him under the cool river water and as he emerged, we were surrounded by brilliant light. I had a vision of the Spirit of God descending upon Jesus like a dove. Then a voice came out of the light, "This is my Son, the Beloved, with whom I am well pleased" (3:17).

He said nothing more after this and walked alone into the wilderness.

That day, I was certain he was the One I had been waiting for. I rejoiced that I had been privileged to witness the Messiah's coming. My waiting had ended. Or, so I thought.

After I met the Messiah, I expected great changes to take place. Because he had come, the pompous high priest would be deposed. The pagan Romans would be expelled from God's land and their idols destroyed. The corrupt Pharisees, scribes, and Sadducees would be driven out of the temple. Through Jesus, God's reign would be established and God's wrath would rain down upon evildoers.

I waited, but none of these things happened. Jesus' coming changed *nothing.* The Romans still ruled and the Pharisees and scribes reigned in the temple. Those who perverted the purposes of God retained power.

I began to have doubts about whether Jesus was truly the Messiah. Then, I was thrown into prison for condemning Herod's immorality with Herodias, his brother's former wife. Here I have had plenty of time to wonder about Jesus.

When my disciples visited not long ago, I begged for news of Jesus. What was he doing? With whom was he traveling? Their answers fanned the flames of my doubts. They reported that Jesus was traveling in the countryside, preaching about God's coming reign and healing the sick. He was doing even less than I did; for I baptized as well!

Instead of wielding a pitchfork to separate the wheat from the chaff, Jesus' hands were curing the infirm, the sick, and the blind. His preaching was more about love and forgiveness than about God's coming wrath. "Could this be the Messiah?" I asked myself.

I am not a subtle man, so I sent my disciples to ask Jesus directly if he is the Messiah. I was very careful in wording the question I sent them to ask: "Are you the Coming One, or are we to wait for another?"

The days I waited for his reply were agonizing. Doubts had chipped away at my belief that Jesus was the Coming One. The vision of the day I baptized Jesus faded to a shadowy dream. Of the great tapestry of hope I began with, I was clinging to a single strand.

Yesterday, they returned. Thaddaeus, the spokesman, said, "Jesus told us to report what we have witnessed. The blind receive their sight, the lame walk, the lepers are cleansed, the deaf hear, the dead are raised, and the poor are hearing good news."

My spirits were beginning to rise from the darkness of despair. Hope was growing within me. "Yes! These are the works of the Messiah foretold by the prophet Isaiah! It is true!" I shouted.

"Did he say anything else?" I asked.

Thaddaeus said, "Just one more thing, but I didn't understand it. 'Blessed is he who takes no offense at me.'"

My face glowed red, because I knew that these words were addressed to me. Instead of condemning me for doubting, Jesus was gracious and forgiving. Remorse over my doubts engulfed me like the waters of the Jordan during a baptism. How could I have ever questioned him? How could my vision have become so clouded? I begged God's forgiveness.

I can now die a contented man. My destiny has been fulfilled. My preaching and baptizing prepared the way for the Coming One. The Messiah has come. God's reign has been established. Evil will be overcome. The waiting is over!

O God, who sent your Son into the world, give me the ability to wait with patience and faith for your coming. When I have doubts, reassure me. When I give in to despair, give me hope. In Jesus' name. Amen.

For Reflection and Discussion

- In what ways can you identify with John's hopes, fears, and doubts?
- How has your understanding of Jesus changed over the years? What caused these changes?
- When have you had to wait for God's reassuring presence? What has given you the strength to wait faithfully?

The Tempter

Read Matthew 4:1-11.

After that pathetic farce called "the baptism," Jesus went into the wilderness to fast and pray. When I found him wandering there, weakened by hunger and exhaustion, I rejoiced that my opportunity had arrived.

You must understand that the wilderness is my domain. I rule this place of savage fear and fierce testing. I am the Master of this great and terrible wasteland, where mortals are most vulnerable. Here they fear dangers, real and imagined that lurk in the shadows and they are worn down by the challenges of survival. When mortals are at their weakest, I am there, for I am the Tempter.

I am known by other names as well: Satan, the Devil, the Adversary, Lucifer, and others. I am nothing like how I am usually portrayed: with horns, a pointed tail, and holding a pitchfork. That is a child's image of Evil, as far from the truth as picturing God as a white-bearded old man sitting on a cloud. I have cultivated this image because it causes mortals to underestimate my power.

I am not a being with mass and form and movement. Rather, I am the Voice of temptation that dwells within. I am the Impulse to choose evil over good, hurt over healing, selfishness over love. I am the Desire to reject and destroy all that is good, true, and worthy. I am the Master of fear, manipulation, and deceit. I am the Tempter.

My power is wielded through two great weapons: intimidation and seduction. Either I compel mortals to choose evil by playing on their fears, or I show them how desirable evil is. Do not belittle the power of these weapons. I win more battles than I lose.

My strategy for crushing the will of Jesus was a twofold assault of intimidation and seduction. If I could convince him to obey me even once, he would be mine.

He was famished, so I first tried to lure him into feeding himself by performing a miracle. I wanted to make him prove to me that he was God's Son. Doing so would elevate his desire to please me over his allegiance to his God. Once he satisfied his hunger at my behest, I would have little trouble convincing him to indulge other desires for pleasure, comfort, power, and wealth. All I needed was a foothold in his soul.

He proved to be a greater adversary than expected. Not only did he refuse to satisfy his hunger with a miracle, he had the audacity to quote unholy scripture to me! I covered my ears, for it pained me to hear it.

"One does not live by bread alone, but by every word that comes from the mouth of God," he said.

Surprised that my first attack was so easily repelled, I launched a more powerful assault. I took Jesus to the pinnacle of the temple and challenged, "If you are the son of God, throw yourself down." Then, I quoted unholy scripture even though it pained me. "It is written, 'He will give his angels charge over you,' and, 'On their hands they will bear you up.'"

I was baiting Jesus into testing his God. If he obeyed me, his soul would be mine. Once persuaded to satisfy his instinct for self-preservation, there would be no end to the desires, wishes, and wants I could convince him to fulfill. If he would indulge my lone request, I would have him under my power.

Unexpectedly, Jesus also resisted the force of this assault and turned me away a second time, quoting unholy scripture: "You shall not tempt the Lord your God."

These words fueled the fires of my rage! No mortal had ever withstood such an onslaught. I could see that the strategy of intimidation wasn't working. So I changed tactics, calling forth the second weapon in my arsenal: seduction.

Again, I took Jesus up to a high place. There, I showed him all the kingdoms of the world and their glory. I offered him their wealth, power, and glory, if he would worship me.

In his depleted condition, I was confident that he would succumb to this magnificent offer. I was certain that he had been weakened by resisting the first two tests.

I was dangling before Jesus nothing less than a position at my right hand. He could have power without pain. I was offering him a way to fulfill his destiny without having to endure the betrayal by Judas, the denial by Peter, and the desertion of his miserable disciples. By worshiping me, he could avoid the agonies that lay ahead: the trial, the beating, the mocking, the scourging, and death by crucifixion. The crown of glory would be his without the cross of suffering. He only had to bow down to me.

Only a fool would turn down this offer. I was certain that the glory of it would overwhelm him. Without hesitating, he ordered me to leave! I was outraged at such arrogance! He had the gall to quote from unholy scripture a third time by saying, "You shall worship the Lord your God and him only shall you serve."

I left in fury, having underestimated him. I immediately began plotting other ways to undo Jesus' trust in his God. I resolved to defeat him through the Sanhedrin who would be threatened by him, through the high priest who would see his power grow, and through the weakness and selfishness of his followers, especially Judas. He won the first battle; I was determined to win the war. He would be mine, or he would die horribly.

Fortunately, most are not like this one called Jesus. Many have been successfully lured away from loyalty to their God. In moments of weakness, I offer mortals a painless and easy way of getting what they want. They nearly always take this easy way. Very few have resisted the urge to follow my way, especially when presented so invitingly. The gods of money, power, and pleasure are worshiped by many. As I said, I win more battles than I lose.

Nothing so undermines my ability to tempt as the repulsive idea of self-giving love that Jesus taught. If I can persuade them to think first of themselves, and of their needs, concerns, and wants, then they will forget about everyone else.

My advice is: Do whatever you must to get what you are entitled to. Strive to achieve wealth, power, and success, no matter who gets hurt. Even more than the gods of wealth, pleasure, and power, worship the god of self. Satisfy your own needs and forget about your neighbor's suffering. Above all, in every situation ask yourself, "What's in this for me?"

If you follow my advice, you and I will be the very best of friends. But, if you choose to follow the way of Jesus, take care, for you, too, may end up on a cross.

Almighty God, who became flesh and was tempted for my sake, strengthen me in times of trial, so that I remain faithful. Give me the courage to resist evil in whatever guise it appears. May I always follow Jesus' way of self-giving love. In Jesus' name I pray. Amen.

For Reflection and Discussion

- When have you faced the temptation to satisfy your physical or emotional hungers at the expense of faithfulness to God?

- From where does Jesus draw his strength to resist temptation? From where do you draw power to resist temptations?
- When have you been offered a painless and easy way to success that would mean a denial of your values? What did you do?

Bleeding Woman

Read Mark 5:24b-34.

If I can just touch him, I will be made well, I say to myself. It is my last hope, my only hope. What is it like to be well? It has been so long that I cannot remember.

Twelve years. Twelve years ago the bleeding started, and it hasn't stopped. Twelve years of watching my life blood seep away like water disappearing into the desert sand. Twelve years of isolation and loneliness.

They call me Bleeding Woman, forgetting that I have a name.

More than anything else, it is the loneliness that wounds. To lose blood is curse enough, but not to be able to touch and be touched, that hurts most of all.

If I can just touch him, I will be made well.

No man will marry an unclean woman; I will never cradle my own child in my arms. An unclean woman is not allowed in the temple. To be unclean is to be untouchable, unlovable, unhuman.

I have sacrificed everything to be healed. Physician after physician has taken my money and left me bleeding, their remedies powerless. Even God has forsaken me.

Countless times I have brought two turtledoves and two pigeons to the priest; a sin offering and a guilt offering have been offered. Are my offerings unclean, too? Will this agony ever be removed from me?

If I can just touch him I will be made well.

I sneak up behind him in the crowd, hoping I won't be recognized as the Bleeding Woman. I follow him like a wolf stalks a lamb. I shove through the mob, but there are so many people and I am not strong. All I can think is, *Get closer, close enough to touch him.*

Suddenly, there is a break in the crowd, and my hand reaches toward his cloak.

If I can just touch him, I will be made well.

At last, my fingers brush against his cloak. I feel the power as it travels up my arm and down deep inside me. Something strange is happening to me. I am drying up! The bleeding has stopped! I am well!

Then the accusation comes. "Who touched me?" he asks. My heart pounds so hard that I am afraid the bleeding will start again. The men with him say, "There are so many pressing near, who *hasn't* touched you?" But I know what he means. He means, Which of the unclean has violated my purity? He means, Who has taken my power without asking?

I throw myself at his feet, careful not to touch him this time. "I touched you," I say, "because I am sick and have bled for twelve years. They call me Bleeding Woman, and I am unclean. I believed that *if I just touched you, I would be made well.* Please forgive me."

Cowering and trembling, I wait for him to take back the gift I stole, and undo the healing. I wait to hear the words of condemnation I have heard so many times. I wait for him to scornfully call me Bleeding Woman, and rush away to wash himself because he was touched by the unclean. I want to cover my ears but do not.

The crowds close in around us like a noose. They will enjoy hearing Jesus rebuke Bleeding Woman. He begins, "Daughter . . . ," but there is no condemnation in his voice! He says, "Daughter, your faith has made you well; go in peace, and be healed of your disease" (v. 34).

He reaches down and gently lifts me to my feet, unafraid to touch the unclean. I am feather light in his hands, ready to float away on the winds of joy. He will not take back the gift of healing; it is mine to keep, forever. No longer am I Bleeding Woman; now I am Daughter of Faith. Able to touch and be touched. Loved and lovable.

I touched him, and I was made well.

Dear Lord, help me to know that you are with me when I am suffering. Give me the courage to reach out to you in hope and need. Let me receive the power of your healing love. In Jesus' name I pray. Amen.

For Reflection and Discussion

- Remember a time when you were very ill. What would it be like to suffer that illness for twelve years?
- In what ways did her frequent bouts of bleeding isolate the woman? What cuts you off from community?
- How does Jesus' healing of this woman have consequences beyond her physical wellness? In what ways does your faith make you well (whole)?

Mary and Martha

Read Luke 10:38-42.

Martha

The day Jesus came to our village was the most memorable of my life.

Mother had been dead for six years, and I was left to take care of Mary and to provide a living for us. I sold our handmade baskets in the market. I loved the market because all the best gossip was shared there first. That's where I learned about the great rabbi named Jesus.

When he walked into our town with his disciples tagging along, the market started buzzing like a beehive. "An amazing teacher," one man said. "He heals the blind and lepers," another added. So many extraordinary things were said about Jesus, I had to see him for myself. I asked Deborah, who sold jewelry in the booth next to me, to watch my baskets while I went to see this great rabbi.

A large crowd had already gathered on the steps of the synagogue when I arrived. Jesus was teaching about the kingdom of God by telling stories. He said God's kingdom was like a woman searching for a lost coin.

This impressed me because I had often turned the house upside down trying to find a lost coin. He then told a story about a man who was left for dead by the side of the road. The man was ignored by a priest and a Levite and was finally helped by a Samaritan. There were murmurs in the crowd after he said, "Go, and do likewise." After all, Samaritans are our enemies.

After he finished teaching, the crowds left to go back to their work and homes. Only a few stragglers remained. On an impulse I went up to Jesus and said, "Master, I would like to invite you to share dinner with my sister and me." He looked pleased to be welcomed into my home. "I would love to come. What is your name?" he said. I replied, "Martha. And please bring your followers, too."

I was so excited about Jesus coming to dinner, I hadn't thought about whether I had enough to feed him and his disciples. I made some quick purchases at the market and ran home. "Mary! The great rabbi, Jesus, is coming to dinner in our home!" I yelled. "Straighten up the house. They'll be here soon."

I was hoping that Mary would pull her weight this time. Since childhood, I had been taking care of her. She was often ill and seemed so fragile. While I didn't mind doing more than my share, sometimes it was too much.

At first, Mary was helpful. She cleaned while I began preparing the meal. Feeding so many is hard work. When Jesus arrived, we both greeted him. I excused myself to the kitchen and expected Mary to follow, but she didn't. She sat down and listened to Jesus teach. I thought that she would sit only a few minutes and then come to help me—preparing supper for so many is too much work for one woman—but she kept sitting. I banged the pots with a ladle, trying to catch my sister's attention. Through the door I could see that she was ignoring me; her gaze was transfixed on Jesus. While I sweated in a hot kitchen, Mary sat with the men.

Finally, I couldn't stand it any longer. The nerve of her, I thought, leaving all the work to me. I was the one who had invited Jesus, not her. She was acting like a guest rather than a hostess. I stomped out of the kitchen and stood before Jesus.

"Lord, do you not care that my sister has left me to do all the work by myself?" I asked.

He replied in a sad, gentle voice, "Martha, Martha, you are worried and distracted by too many things. Only one thing is important and Mary has realized it."

Openmouthed, I stood as rigid as a pillar. The great rabbi had taken my sister's side! I couldn't speak. I wanted to crawl out of the room. Humiliated, I went back into the kitchen.

Mary

When Jesus came to our home at my sister's invitation, I didn't know what to expect. I had heard of his reputation as a great teacher and healer. It was said that crowds flocked around him like sheep to a shepherd. If anyone could muster the nerve to ask this great rabbi to dinner, it was Martha.

Since childhood, Martha had been stronger than me. As the older daughter, she assumed more than her share of duties and chores, and let me know it. I was ill much of the time as a child. Mother said that I had almost died at birth. Maybe her attention to my illness bordered on coddling, but when I objected, she responded, "I'm so grateful you're alive at all."

I knew Martha resented the attention Mother gave me, even when I was so sick that I couldn't feed myself. Occasionally, she cast angry glares in my direction when Mother wasn't looking. Once, she teased me, calling me "the baby." Of course, children do such things.

When we were adults, Martha no longer teased, but I could tell she still thought of me as a weak and fragile child. Over my protests she insisted on doing a greater share of the household work. I think she needed to be in control.

Living with her was challenging, but I had no choice. As the elder, she had received most of the meager inheritance left by Mother. Neither of us remembered our father who died when we were very young. Marriage, the only way to be free of Martha, was not possible for me until she married. Unfortunately, Martha had no prospects. Her sharp tongue and brusque manner put off any potential suitors. To earn enough to live, we shared expenses by selling the baskets we made. Neither of us could make ends meet alone.

On those warm Galilean nights, I would lie awake dreaming of a different life, filled with love and laughter and children. I would imagine myself living in my own home with a husband who adored me. Most of all, I would dream of being on my own.

I remembered my dream when Jesus walked into the room. Just to be in his presence was refreshing. When he spoke, all I wanted to do was listen. He described the kingdom of God like it was already here. Using stories and parables, he talked about God's love and forgiveness.

Entranced, I sat at his feet, my entire being absorbing his words. I could not have moved from that spot even if I wanted to. It was as if I had grown roots into the floor and had sprung leaves to take in the nourishment of his teachings.

As I listened, I was vaguely aware of my sister preparing for supper. She was making a great deal of noise, hoping to be noticed. Finally, she burst into the room and said in exasperation, "Lord, do you not care that my sister has left me to do all the work by myself?"

I was shocked that she would address Jesus in such a tone. I started to rise off the floor, bracing myself for Jesus' rebuke. To my astonishment, he said, "Martha, Martha, you are worried and distracted by too many things. Only one thing is important and Mary has realized it."

Never had I felt freer than in that moment. Instead of making me feel guilty about sitting and listening, Jesus affirmed me. Somehow, I had done the right thing without realizing it.

Though vindicated by Jesus, I felt pity for Martha. She was only doing what she had always done: taking care of her guests. Jesus was right, however: she was worried and distracted. Those two words captured her spirit.

For the first time in my life, I felt stronger than Martha. Jesus had blessed my choice. I pray that Martha, too, will one day realize the one, most important thing.

Dear Lord, there are so many distractions from the one, most important thing. Help me to see that living for you is my highest purpose. May I sit at your feet and hear the words of truth that lead to new life. In Jesus' name I pray. Amen.

For Reflection and Discussion

- With whom do you identify more: Martha or Mary? Why?
- Why does Jesus affirm Mary's choice, while challenging Martha's? When have you been confronted with a decision like the one they faced?
- In what areas of your life can you choose to listen to God's guidance more intently and follow Jesus more faithfully?

Zacchaeus

Read Luke 19:1-10.

Being a tax collector is no picnic. Of all the creatures the Lord God put on this earth, tax collectors are the most hated. We are despised and degraded more than all other so-called sinners—even prostitutes and adulterers. And why? For doing our jobs.

The problem is that we work for the Roman oppressors. But somebody has to do the unpleasant jobs. Would my fellow Jews rather have a Roman collecting their tribute or a sympathetic countryman?

Of the tax collectors in Palestine, I am the most scorned. My prosperity has led everyone to conclude that I am dishonest. I admit to a few *minor* improprieties, like cheating some of the wealthier landowners—who, I might add, were trying to cheat me first. But I've never swindled the poor. Frankly, I am the victim of cheating far more often than I am the culprit. Some rabbis even say that it is permissible to lie to a tax collector!

You think I wanted to become a tax collector? It definitely wasn't my first choice for a profession. I would have preferred being a farmer like my father. As a farmer, I would have been respected by my peers and accepted in the Temple. Alas, I was too short to farm. I tried plowing, but couldn't see over the donkey's hind end. My father laughed at the zigzag furrows I plowed. When harvesttime came, I was too small to lift the large bundles of wheat onto the donkeys' backs. Those watching would tease me saying, "Little Zac-chaeus. A boy can't do a man's job."

After enduring years of mockery because of my size, I vowed that someday I would show everyone that smallness of stature is not a barrier to abundance of power. The pursuit of power led me to apply for the job of tax collector. In taking this job that nobody wanted, I knew I would be disliked. But, I would also have all the power that money can buy.

As a tax collector I advanced quickly because of shrewd-ness and hard work. My district, Jericho, was fertile soil for crops and collections. It wasn't long before I became a wealthy citizen. People talked about me, behind my back of course, but if they didn't respect me, at least they feared me.

Strangely, despite my wealth and high rank, I was un-happy. I longed to be accepted for myself rather than because of my money. Dissatisfied and unfulfilled, I realized that power purchased by wealth wasn't enough.

One day I heard that a great rabbi was coming to Jericho. Jesus was said to he a healer and wise teacher. Some even wondered if he was the Messiah. I was almost sick with curiosity about Jesus. I wanted to see him nearly as badly as I wanted to be a foot taller.

The day he arrived in Jericho, crowds gathered on both sides of the main road, creating a human wall that I couldn't break through. I heard those in the front say, "He's coming! Look, there he is!" Desperate to get a glimpse of this rabbi, I glanced to the left and right looking for a way. Suddenly, I saw it! A sycamore tree up the road about a hundred feet. I ran behind the crowds and scaled the tree just in time. Jesus was passing by, followed by several ordinary-looking men.

To my amazement, Jesus stopped and looked up. I was so shocked that I nearly lost my grip. There were gasps from the crowd below when I slipped.

Jesus' voice floated up to me as if in a dream. "Zacchaeus," he said. *How did he know my name?* "Hurry and come down;

for I must stay at your house today" (v. 5). This had to be a dream. Why would he want to stay at *my* house?

I scrambled down so quickly I almost fell a second time. This great rabbi had asked to stay at *my* house! Of all the citizens of Jericho, I was chosen for this honor. Joy welled up within me like a gushing spring. Jesus would be dining with me, Zacchaeus the tax collector. For the first time in my life, I felt accepted.

From the crowd around me came rumbles, like the growling of an angry dog. One man sneered, "Jesus is going to be the guest of a sinner!" Another added, "The chief sinner and a traitor." So great was my joy that the jeers of the crowd didn't distress me.

Suddenly, my joy withered as quickly as it had sprouted. *I am unworthy,* I thought. *I do not deserve to be in the presence of this man of God. The voices from the crowd are right. I am the chief sinner; a betrayer of my own people.* The weight of years of dishonesty suddenly bore down upon me until I was nearly crushed by guilt.

The only way I could accept Jesus' request to come to my house was to atone for the evil I had done. I saw the angry faces of those I had cheated over the years looking down on me from the surrounding crowd. I also saw the tired and hungry faces of the wretched poor. My wealth began to suffocate me. I felt that I must shed it like a caterpillar's cocoon if I was to host Jesus.

I heard myself saying, "Lord, I will give half of my possessions to the poor. And I will pay back those I have cheated four times the amount." It was as if another man had spoken the words. The old Zacchaeus would never have made such a rash and unselfish vow.

Jesus' reply confirmed my transformation. "Today salvation has come to this house, because he too is a son of Abraham. For the Son of Man came to seek out and to save the lost" (vv. 9-10).

I glowed with the warmth of one who has started a new life. I could scarcely believe what Jesus has called me: a son of Abraham. For so many years I had been a traitor to my heritage. I had sought acceptance through wealth and power, at the expense of self-respect. Instead of cheating others, I had been cheating myself.

Now I was home. Salvation was coming to my house and its name was Jesus. For the first time in my life, I felt tall.

Dear Lord, forgive me when feelings of insecurity cause me to build myself up at the expense of others. Remind me that stature is not measured by wealth or power, but by love and compassion. May your salvation come to my house this very day. In Jesus' name I pray. Amen.

For Reflection and Discussion

- How did Zacchaeus deal with his feelings of inadequacy? When have you felt inadequate and how did you cope with this?
- How did Zacchaeus' encounter with Jesus change him? When have you had a life-changing encounter with Jesus?
- What did Jesus mean when he said, "Today salvation has come to this house"?
- How would you react to Jesus coming to your house? What would you need to do to get ready for his visit?

The Man Born Blind

Read John 9.

I am begging by the side of the road, just as I have done since childhood, when I hear footsteps approach.

"Alms for a blind man," I call out.

One of the voices asks gruffly, "How do we know this beggar is truly blind?"

"I have been blind from birth, good sir. Ask anyone who lives here," I say.

Another voice asks, "Rabbi, who sinned, this man or his parents, that he was born blind?" I bristle at this question but hold my tongue, hoping that my patience will be rewarded with a few shackels.

"Neither sinned," the rabbi says. "He was born blind so that God's works might be revealed." I like the strong and compassionate voice of the rabbi even though I don't know what he means about God's works. He adds, "As long as I am in the world, I am the light of the world."

I am puzzled by his words, but my thoughts are diverted by the sound of someone spitting. Soon I feel warm mud being spread on my sightless eyes. It feels soothing even if it is made from spittle. Then the rabbi says, "Go and wash in the pool of Siloam." His voice is so compelling, I immediately leap up and tap my way to the legendary pool.

An astonishing thing happens when I wash the mud from my eyes. I begin to see shapes of light for the first time! The shapes become clearer and more defined. Images become sharp and colorful. In amazement, I see faces of people for the first time in my life! I dance with joy in the street like a crazy man. "I can see," I yell. "I can see!"

Thrilled, I run home. It feels strange to see the way rather than to feel it. As I run and sing my neighbors came out to see what the commotion is about. At first, some don't believe I am the same blind man who sits begging by the road each day. I assure them that I am and call them by name. Some finally believe me, and ask, "How were your eyes opened?" I tell them, "The man called Jesus made mud, spread it on my eyes, and told me to wash in the pool of Siloam. When I washed, I received my sight!" They ask me where he is but I do not know.

One of my neighbors must have gossiped to the Pharisees about my miracle because I am hauled in for questioning later that day. "Come with us," one of the temple guards says roughly as he shoves me toward the temple.

Several bearded, stern-looking Pharisees are gathered in one of the chambers of the temple. They ask how I received my sight and I tell them the same story that I told my neighbors. Some Pharisees are upset that Jesus healed me on the Sabbath while others object, "How can a sinner perform such signs?" An argument arises between the two groups and becomes loud and heated. Finally, one of them turns to me and asks, "What do you say about him?" Without thinking I blurt out, "He is a prophet."

After my outburst, a few of them question whether I was really blind in the first place. Pharisees are born cynics. "Ask my parents, if you don't believe me," I say.

Cowering, my father and mother are brought before the interrogators. The power of the Sanhedrin is the cause of their shaking hands and averted eyes.

"Is this your son, who you say was born blind?" one of them skeptically asks my parents.

"Y-y-y-es, s-s-sir," my father stammers.

"How then does he now see?" the Pharisee sneers.

My father answers as if he were on trial, "All we know is that he was born blind. How he now sees and who opened his eyes, we do not know. Ask him, he is old enough to speak for himself." He is afraid to mention the name of Jesus. Father has heard rumors that Jesus' followers are being cast out of the synagogues.

After my parents are allowed to leave, I am questioned a second time.

"Give glory to God! We know that this man is a sinner," my interrogator claims.

"I do not know whether he is a sinner. All I know is that I was blind and now I see," I say.

Like my parents, I don't want to be excommunicated from the synagogue. Yet, I am irritated by the accusing tone of their questions. Not only do they doubt my honesty, they are trying to discredit the prophet Jesus who gave me my sight.

"Tell us again how he opened your eyes and what he did to you," they command.

Irritation boils over into anger. "I have told you several times and you will not listen. Why do you want to hear my story again? Do you also want to become his disciples?"

Immediately after I say this, I regret it. They are enraged by the suggestion they might become followers of Jesus.

They yell venomously, "You are his disciple, but we are disciples of Moses. We know that God has spoken to Moses, but we do not know where this man comes from."

Summoning my courage I say, "Here is an amazing thing! You do not know where he comes from and yet he opened my eyes. We know that God doesn't listen to sinners, but listens to those who worship him and obey his will. Never since the beginning of the world has it been heard that anyone opened the eyes of a man born blind. If this man Jesus were not from God, he could do nothing."

I have pushed them too far. They begin beating me and spit on me. As I flee from the temple I hear one of them scream, "You were born entirely in sin, and you are trying to teach us?"

Free from my inquisitors I wander the streets aimlessly. The interrogation has diminished the joy of receiving my sight. I worry that word will soon spread about my being driven out of the temple. I am concerned about where I will live. If I am excommunicated, I will be seen as unclean by my neighbors and friends. I smile at the irony: as a blind man I was an outcast; my healing has made me an outcast a second time.

Suddenly, I hear a voice from behind me ask, "Do you believe in the Son of Man?"

I recognize the voice as that of the rabbi Jesus. I turn around and look upon my healer. His question strikes me as strange. Since boyhood I have heard about the Son of Man who will come from heaven and establish justice upon the earth. Some rabbis preach that the Son of Man will come in our generation.

"And who is he, sir, that I may believe in him?" I ask.

"The one speaking with you is he," Jesus says.

Overcome by wonder and awe I say, "Lord, I believe."

I fall down at the Lord's feet and worship him. Even though my eyes are open, until now I did not see who this man Jesus truly is. Once he revealed himself as the Son of Man, it is as if I receive my sight a second time.

I begin to realize that everyone is blind until they see the Truth. Jesus' disciples were blind because they mistakenly thought my blindness was caused by sin. My neighbors were blind with skepticism and disbelief. My parents were blinded by their fear of the Pharisees. And the Pharisees were the blindest of all because they didn't believe in Jesus.

Jesus continues, "I came into this world for judgment so that those who do not see may see, and those who do see may become blind."

Some Pharisees who have been following him overhear this and ask, "Surely we are not blind, are we?"

Jesus says, "If you were blind, you would not have sin. But because you claim to see, your sin remains."

They jump up and down with rage. Jesus leaves them wallowing in their wrath. He has spoken the truth: those who think they are without sin are in the deepest darkness of all. The Pharisees claim to see the "truth" that Jesus is a sinner. In pronouncing judgment on Jesus, the Son of Man, they judge themselves. There are none so blind as those who refuse to see.

I now see the meaning of one of the first things I heard Jesus say, about being the "light of the world." He is the one who was sent by God to illumine the truth about each person. As we stand in the light of his judgment, we see ourselves as we truly are. And, when we truly see, we fall down and worship Jesus, Son of Man and Son of God.

To receive one's sight is a glorious thing. To receive the sight called "faith" is even more magnificent.

Almighty God, who sent your Light into the world, please illumine me so that I am able to see the Truth. Let me not shrink away from the fact that I am a sinner redeemed by a Savior's love. May the light of your presence kindle in me a glowing faith. In Jesus' name I pray. Amen.

For Reflection and Discussion

- What forms of "blindness" exhibited by the characters in this story do you have?
- How does the blind man progressively move from sight to insight? When has the Truth enabled you to see yourself clearly?
- What does Jesus' statement, "I am the light of the world," mean to you? What are the connections between sight and faith?

Lazarus

Read John 11:1-44.

The light hurts. The brightness sears my eyes. I recoil from the painful brilliance. I want to stay in the cool and soothing darkness. Where am I? What is this place of darkness with light blazing through the doorway? Why are these cloths wrapped around me? And that smell. What is that awful stench? Am I in a dream or a nightmare?

I remember. I was ill. My fever rose and I saw only blackness. How long have I been asleep? A day, a year, an eternity? Time seems to have stopped.

I hear my name. "Lazarus, come out!" I am summoned into the burning light. That voice. Where have I heard the voice calling me out of the darkness?

My eyes gradually adjust to the light. I see indistinct shapes and blurred forms, like mirages shimmering on the horizon. I hear the voices of women. They also are vaguely familiar.

One shape comes into focus. A man standing apart from the crowd. His silhouette is familiar. I begin walking into the glaring brightness. People are all around. They turn their heads and cover their noses. I hear someone vomit. I smell myself. The putrid odor is coming from me!

A terrible awareness dawns upon my dulled senses. I am wrapped in grave clothes. My flesh is rotting. I reek of death. *Am I dead?*

I remember the burning fever, my sister Martha weeping and saying, "He is dying." I must have died! But that is impossible!

Now I am alive! Called out of death by the voice of . . . Jesus. Yes, it is Jesus' voice who called me out of a . . . tomb. I don't remember being placed there. I was dead then. I am alive! How can this be?

This is too much for me to take in. I am overwhelmed with . . . Joy? Confusion? Wonder? Fear? Yes. All of these and more. Words cannot capture the emotions I feel.

Am I really alive? I try to remember what life feels like. To live is to see, smell, and walk. I try to speak, but cannot. Something is wrapped around my jaw keeping my mouth closed. I try to unwrap the cloths binding me but cannot. I feel my own touch! I hear myself breathing. I really am alive!

A question burns within. Why did Jesus do it? Why was the darkness of death disturbed by the light of life? I don't deserve a second life. One life is all that God allots mortals. "Why me?" I want to ask him, but he is busy speaking to the astonished crowd. I take a step toward them and they cower. They look as if they have seen a spirit. Am I a spirit? No. I feel my flesh. I move my leaden legs as if I had awakened from a long sleep.

Two women come toward me holding the hem of their robes over their noses like masks. I can see only their eyes. I know those eyes. Mary! Martha! I try to speak their names, but my jaw is still bound. I try to embrace them, but they recoil. Even they cannot stand the stench. I, too, would flee from this odor if I could.

I hear Jesus' command, "Unbind him and let him go." I fumble with the cloth around my jaw and feel it loosen. My sisters start unwrapping my grave clothes. I will be naked, but what do I care? A naked dead man who has come to life! What a story these people will have to tell.

Almighty God, who raised Lazarus from death to life, I confess that I have preferred the comfort of darkness to the exposure of light. Give me the ears to hear your summons to new life. Give me the courage to walk out of my self-made tombs of fear, alienation, and selfishness into the light of your love. Amen.

For Reflection and Discussion

- When has the power of God's love brought you out of a self-made tomb of fear, guilt, addiction, or selfishness?
- How does the sign of Lazarus' raising show you that Jesus is the Resurrection and the Life?
- In what ways is God calling you from death to new life in the present moment?

Mary of Bethany

Read John 11:28-37; 12:1-8.

I am busy in the kitchen with Martha when the Lord walks through the door. My brother rushes to greet him and I quickly follow. Suddenly, the room seems brighter, more joyous. Seeing Lazarus and the Lord embrace takes me back to a day I will never forget.

Martha has just burst into the house telling me, "The Teacher is here and is calling for you." I leap to my feet and run to him as if I am in a race. I can barely hold back the tears that are threatening to begin again. When I see him, I fall down and wet his feet with my tears. "Lord, if you had been here, my brother would not have died," I say through the sobs. My brother has been dead four days! The thought that the Lord didn't come in time to prevent his death adds bitterness to my sorrow. Now, Martha and I are alone.

Seeing the Lord again releases powerful feelings within me: overwhelming joy, overflowing gratitude, overpowering love. I can never repay him for the gift of life he gave. My beloved brother has been given back to me. There is no repaying this priceless gift.

After the Lord raises me to my feet I can see that he is deeply distressed. I try to stop crying so I won't upset him, but the tears keep flowing. "Where have you laid him?" he asks. My friends who have followed me say, "Come and see." Now the Lord has joined our tearful mourning. We walk toward the tomb in a procession of grief.

As I look upon the Lord a sense of danger seizes me. He risks too much by coming here. The Pharisees want to arrest him; they have given orders that anyone knowing his whereabouts must alert them. But no furrows of worry crease his brow.

When everyone finally reclines around the table, Martha begins serving. Her gift to the Lord is this supper. She has been preparing it for three days, ever since she heard that the Lord might visit. In her own way, she is as grateful to him as I am. I help her serve. My brother is sitting to the right of the Lord, aglow with joy.

When we come to the tomb, the Lord shudders. He is still deeply disturbed and looks down at his feet. Martha and the others are there also, having heard that the Lord will pay his final respects to his friend and our brother.

"Take away the stone," he commands. Gasps can be heard among the crowd. Martha says what all of us are afraid to utter.

"Lord, he has been dead four days and there will be a stench."

The Lord replies, "Did I not tell you that if you believed, you would see the glory of God?"

After Martha and I serve at table, I am trembling. I, too, want to give the Lord a gift. With all my love, I want to give him the most precious thing I possess: an entire pound of expensive nard. I am nervous about what he will say about such extravagance, but I lift the jar containing the perfume from the wicker basket under the table.

The talking stops as I pour the perfumed oil over the Lord's feet. The oil caresses his feet so slowly and gently; rivulets of perfume glide across his skin and drip onto the fabric of the chair. The fragrance of the perfume fills the house and flows out the open window.

They are rolling away the stone and we cover our faces with the hems of our robes. The Lord looks up at the sky and prays, "Father, I thank you for having heard me. I knew that you always hear me, but I have said this for the sake of the crowd standing here, so that they may believe that you sent me."

Then the Lord cries out with a thunderous voice, "Lazarus, come out!"

The gift of perfume isn't enough. I want, I need, I must express my gratitude to and love for the Lord with an extraordinary gesture. So I loosen my hair from its tight ball, bend down over the Lord's feet and lovingly wipe the perfume from them. My face is afire when I realize what I am doing, but I am safely hidden by my hair.

A voice of outrage interrupts my offering. "Why was this perfume not sold for three hundred denarii and the money given to the poor?" Judas owns the voice.

I draw back from the Lord's feet as if they are two serpents. Judas is right! I shouldn't have performed this lavish, wasteful act. I should have found another, more acceptable way to show my love. I have humiliated the Lord and myself. I am poised to throw myself on the floor and beg his forgiveness when the Lord speaks.

"Leave her alone. She bought it so that she might keep it for the day of my burial. You will always have the poor with you, but you do not always have me."

At the Lord's command, my brother walks out of the tomb. I push back the hair from my eyes and stare in joy and disbelief. For four days I have grieved his death; now I am celebrating his second life. "Unbind him, and let him go," the Lord says. Martha and I run to him and begin to unbind our brother who is now free of death, free to live and love.

Why is the Lord speaking of his death? I didn't mean for the perfume to be used for his burial. A sense of sadness and loss so overwhelms me that I feel my knees buckle. I reach out and clutch the table so that I won't collapse. Then a thought, consoling and uplifting, arises within me: if the Lord can raise my brother from the dead, there is no limit to his power over death! The Lord told Martha before raising our brother: "I am the resurrection and the life."

The luscious scent of perfume demands my attention. In the fragrance is the aroma of gratitude, of love, and of life that never ends.

Lord of Life, may I always be grateful for your gift of life and new life. Show me ways to express my love for you by serving others. Help me to be generous with my gifts, always willing to share them. In Jesus' name I pray. Amen.

For Reflection and Discussion

- Why is Mary so grateful to Jesus? For what are you thankful to God?
- How is Mary's anointing of Jesus an act of love? How do you show gratitude to God?
- Was her gift too expensive and wasteful? Why or why not?
- How does Mary unknowingly prepare Jesus for the day of his burial?

Act III
Jesus' Passion

Judas Iscariot

Read Matthew 16:13-23; 21:1-11; 26:6-56; 27:3-5.

Before I tell you my name, you must promise to hear me out. Too many have condemned my treachery before hearing my side of the story. My name? Judas Iscariot. I have been called many cruel and hateful names as well: Murderer, Betrayer, Christ Killer, Traitor, and Satan.

It is easy to forget that I was one of the chosen Twelve. The Master called me to be in his inner circle of followers. As the only Judean among the Twelve, I stood apart from the others, alone and isolated. The others were jealous of me because I was the treasurer for our group, a position of great trust and honor.

I took care of the money (there was never much) for our small fellowship. What little we had, I conserved with great care. Frugality, not miserliness, was my way.

When the woman poured an expensive oil over the Master's head, I, along with James and John, protested that this gesture was far too extravagant. And it was. The ointment could have sold for three hundred denarii, an entire year's wages for a laborer! That amount would have fed hundreds of the city's poor. As treasurer, I had a responsibility to use a portion of our funds for those in need. The Master had a special love for the poor. I was just doing my job in objecting to this waste.

I didn't understand why we were rebuked by the Master. With quiet anger he said, "Leave her alone. You will always have the poor with you, but you will not always have me. She has prepared me for burial." None of us understood what he meant about his burial, until later.

How can I describe the Master? He was demanding, yet compassionate; soft-spoken, yet powerful. When I followed him, I knew it was for the rest of my life. Like the eleven others, I left everything for him: my home, my parents, my trade as a merchant of fine goods.

The longer I was with the Master, the more I began to suspect that he was the long-awaited Messiah. His preaching, his healing, and, most of all, his teaching, led me to this conclusion. He proclaimed the coming kingdom of God, a kingdom my people had longed for. I desperately hoped he was the One sent by God to break the yoke of oppression forced on us by the Roman dogs.

One day, as we were walking from Bethsaida to the villages of Caesarea Philippi, the Master asked us, "Who do the people say that I am?"

Philip answered, "John the Baptist."

James said, "Elijah."

John said, "One of the prophets."

Then, the Master asked, "But who do you say that I am?"

Peter blurted out, "You are the Messiah."

None of us were prepared for what followed. The Master swore us to secrecy, as if to confirm our belief. Then he began to teach us about the fate of the Messiah, whom he said would undergo terrible suffering, be rejected, killed, and rise on the third day.

All of us were shocked at the thought that the Messiah would die. Peter took the Master aside and began to object heatedly. The Master turned, looked at all of us, and said to Peter, "Get behind me, Satan! You are a stumbling block to me; for you are setting your mind not on divine things but on human things." After this, we were afraid to answer the Master's questions.

How can I make you believe that I loved the Master more than I can express? My love was returned a hundred-fold by the Master. Not only did he love us, he loved everyone: babies, children, the aged, the sick, the infirm and diseased. He would talk with anyone, no matter who they were: prostitutes, tax collectors, and even Samaritans. He treated everyone with compassion, except those who were self-righteous. With hypocrites he had no patience.

When the priests sent out their spies to trick the Master into committing blasphemy, he turned their words back on them, making them look foolish. I wondered why he put up with their silly games. He could destroy them with one word, if he chose to.

The Master was the most unique man I had ever known. I eventually came to believe with all my heart that he was the Messiah, God's very own Son. To see him was to see God.

Do you think I could have betrayed this man whom I loved so deeply? What I did wasn't betrayal in my eyes. I had a plan, a very clever scheme, that began to take shape just before Passover. The Master had been gaining in popularity with the common people. Larger and larger crowds were coming to hear his teaching and to be healed of every kind of infirmity. As his popularity grew, so did his power. He had become a threat to the high priests and the ruling council. They sought a way to arrest him. I smiled at the pitiful delusion that they had any power over the Master. He was the Messiah! God's Son! One word from him and the Lord would send legions of angels to destroy these petty men with their pathetic plans to hurt the Master.

On the first day of the week before Passover, I saw my hope for the Master seizing his destiny begin to be fulfilled. He rode into Jerusalem on a colt like the great kings of old. Thousands gathered along the side of the road and began to spread palm branches and garments on the road in adoration. Spontaneous cheers broke out. "Hosanna!" the crowd shouted. What was happening went beyond my most fervent dreams. I was certain that the Master would ride to Herod's palace in Jerusalem and take his rightful place on the throne. This was the moment when he would establish his rightful place as King and Messiah! Or, so I thought.

To my everlasting disappointment, after he entered the city, he got off the colt and walked away from the crowd. He had them in the palm of his hand, but let them slip from his grasp! At his command, they would have stormed the palace. Unbelievably, no command was given. I was stunned.

I caught a glimpse of his face as he disappeared into the crowds. I had seen that look before. The Master wore an expression of pity, as if nobody understood him or his kingdom.

In a daze of distress, I decided, "If he won't take his place on the throne, then I will force the issue." I initiated a plan devised to compel the Master to claim his rightful position on Herod's throne. I believed that, with the right kind of encouragement, he would exercise his God-given power to destroy his enemies and establish his reign.

So, I went to the priests who were so anxious to arrest him. I told them that I would turn the Master over to them on the night of Passover. To convince them, I requested payment. They offered the trivial sum of thirty pieces of silver, which I immediately accepted. I played the part of the traitor well.

As I deceived these fools, I laughed inwardly at their gullibility. They imagined that if they could catch the Master away from the crowds, they could subdue him and defeat him. What idiots!

On the night of Passover, thirteen of us shared our meal in a room on the second floor of an obscure house in Jerusalem. The tone of the meal was somber, unlike so many of the joyous meals we had shared together. When the Master broke the bread, he said it was his body. After supper was finished he took a cup of wine and said that it was his blood. None of us understood his words, but we didn't dare ask what he meant.

Then he said, "One of you will betray me."

Several asked, "Is it I?"

He said, "The one who has dipped his hand into the bowl with me will betray me." I saw my hand next to his. Our eyes met briefly and I left in confusion and fear. The Master knew everything about us; he must know of my plan, I thought. Is he giving me permission to carry it out? I got up from the table and went to the priests. The others thought that I had gone to buy more food.

Later that night, I led the priests and their soldiers to the garden on the Mount of Olives where I knew he would be praying. Since they weren't sure what the Master looked like, and because of the darkness, I marked him with a kiss. The look on his face pierced me like a sword. He looked betrayed. In horror, I realized that I had made a horrible and tragic mistake.

The Master didn't lift a hand to protect himself. Like a sheep being led to slaughter, he went without a struggle. When I realized that he would not save himself, I knew that he would die.

I was in agony over what I had done. I saw my error too late. The Master was indeed a king, but had no interest in ruling Jerusalem or even Israel. His kingdom was not of this world. He was the king of love. How could I have been so blind? He was telling us this truth all along, but I couldn't see it. His was not a political kingdom, but the reign of God.

The Master's entire life was one of loving service. He sought no power for himself. He cared nothing for power that was not rooted in love. In pure love, he submitted to a cross of death.

As I gazed at the rope I would use to hang myself, I had no fear of death. I simply could not live with what I had done. If the Master was going to die, I would join him. I was not afraid because I knew that the Master would forgive me, had already forgiven me. I could not forgive myself.

Almighty God, who sent Jesus to give himself for me, forgive my betrayals of him. Forgive my selfishness, my desire for power, my willingness to place pleasure above pleasing you. May I demonstrate my acceptance of your forgiveness by forgiving myself. In Jesus' name I pray. Amen.

For Reflection and Discussion

- Where do you agree or disagree with Judas' justification of his betrayal of Jesus in this account?
- What motives of his actions does Judas reveal in the story? When have mixed motives led you to hurt someone you love?
- When has God's forgiveness of you enabled you to forgive yourself or another person? What did you have to let go of to accept God's forgiveness?
- Who have been the Judases in your life? Are you able to forgive them?

Peter the Denier

Read John 1:35-42; 13; 18:1-27.

When Andrew stood on the shore waving his arms wildly and shouting, "We have found the Messiah," I thought he was possessed by a deranged spirit. I was wrestling with a full net on a scorching Galilean day; steam was rising from the lake. Fishing is backbreaking labor, especially when working alone, and I was suffering from the blistering heat.

I had been alone for two months because my brother Andrew was off on his latest quest to find the Messiah. Since childhood he dreamed of finding the Anointed One whom our people longed for. His dream was my nightmare.

Two months ago, word reached us that a man named John was baptizing in the Jordan River a few miles away.

"Please, Simon, let me go and see if he's the One. I'll come back and help you once I've seen him," he said.

"I've heard this before, little brother. You go off chasing each new Messiah and I get stuck with the work."

"Simon, this will be the last time. I have a feeling about John the Baptizer. He may really be the One."

Even though I thought he was crazy, I let him go, as usual.

After he left, I didn't hear a word from Andrew until he showed up, yelling on the shore. Since it was the last catch of the day, I emptied the net into the hold and rowed to shore. Andrew was waiting impatiently, hopping from one leg to the other.

"Simon! Simon! I have found him!"

"How can you be sure?" I asked.

"I've never been so certain of anything! Come with me, now! I'll take you to him!"

"Are you crazy? Look at all the fish that have to be cleaned and salted for market tomorrow. You've been away so long you've forgotten how to work."

"The fish can wait! Come, you must see the Messiah for yourself!"

To shut Andrew up I said, "You help me with the fish and then I'll go and see your so-called Messiah."

"Done!"

Andrew worked like a man possessed, which I suspected he was, and the fish were soon prepared. Not taking time to wash, Andrew hurriedly led me to meet his latest Messiah. We stank of fish entrails.

Along the road to Bethany, Andrew told his story.

"I was with John, listening to his teachings, and up walks this man who looks like a common laborer. John says, 'Look, here is the Lamb of God.' That's John's word for Messiah. Thomas and I follow this stranger for awhile. Then he turns and asks, 'What are you looking for?' as if he could see into our hearts and know our innermost thoughts. I ask, 'Rabbi, where are you staying?' and he replies, 'Come and see.' I knew he was the Anointed One not only because of what John said, but because of his teachings. Simon, you must see him for yourself."

We arrived at our destination and Andrew took me to a man he called Jesus of Nazareth. Andrew was right; he looked common. My impression of him changed when he stared at me intensely and said, "You are Simon son of John. You are to be called Cephas."

I was astonished at the boldness of this man I had never met. It was as if he already knew me. He called me "Cephas," which in my language means "rock." All who know me well would understand that Cephas was the perfect name for me.

I was as stubborn and hardheaded as a rock. Once I made up my mind I acted, often without thinking.

What better way to start a new life than with a new name? Without hesitation, I joined my brother and followed Jesus.

* * * * * * * * * * * * * *

The room was dark, giving it a gloomy feeling. We were gathered for a meal on the eve of Passover. Because the Lord was quietly pensive, we ate in silence. During supper, he stood, removed his robe and tied a towel around his waist like a servant. He poured water into a clay basin and began to wash the feet of each of us, drying them with the towel. "This is slave's work," I thought. I couldn't imagine the Lord, the One we believed to be the Messiah, doing the work of a common slave.

When he knelt at my feet, I asked, "Lord, are you going to wash my feet, too?"

He said, "You do not know now what I am doing, but later you will understand."

I said firmly, "You will never wash my feet."

The Lord's tone matched mine: "Unless I wash you, you will have no future with me."

"Then wash not only my feet, but my whole body," I said.

After washing my feet, the Lord said, "Not all of you are clean." I was puzzled by this.

He continued teaching, as he often did after performing a sign, "If I, your Lord and Master, wash your feet, you also ought to wash one another's feet. I have done this as an example for you."

At the time I thought, "How strange to tell us to wash each other's feet." Later I realized that he was not talking about foot washing, but about love. We were to follow his example and lovingly serve one another. As with everything the Lord did, foot washing pointed to a deeper truth.

After the foot washing we gathered around the table for supper. The Lord's face darkened with an expression I had never seen. He looked deeply distressed, as if in pain.

"I tell you truly, one of you will betray me," he said. I glanced at Andrew whose expression was a mixture of horror and sadness. "Who could he mean?" I thought. I turned to John, who was sitting next to Jesus, and whispered, "Ask him who he means."

John asked and the Lord said, "The one to whom I'm giving this piece of bread dipped in the dish." He handed the bread to Judas and said, "Do quickly what you must."

We thought Judas was simply leaving to buy more food. He was the treasurer and often left a meal early to buy food for the next day.

With Judas gone in the darkness of night, the Lord continued teaching, "Little children, I am with you only a little longer. You will look for me, but where I am going, you cannot come."

Immediately I asked, "Lord, where are you going?"

He said, "You cannot follow me now where I am going, but you will follow afterward."

I was confused and afraid as I said, "Lord why can't I follow you now? I would lay down my life for you."

Shaking his head slowly from side to side, he answered, "Will you lay down your life for me? In truth, before the cock crows, you will have denied me three times."

The mystery of where Judas went was soon solved. After supper, we went with the Lord across the Kidron valley to a garden where he liked to pray. While we were praying, Judas emerged from the shadows leading a group made up of Roman soldiers, chief priests' guards, and some Pharisees.

The Lord turned and asked, "Whom are you looking for?"

They replied, "Jesus of Nazareth."

When the Lord said, "I am he," they stepped back and fell to the ground. He asked them a second time whom were they seeking. Their answer was the same. "You have found me. Now, let these men go," he said.

I couldn't allow the Lord to be arrested without a fight. I drew a sword from under my cloak and slashed at the man who was about to seize the Lord, cutting off his ear. The Lord rebuked me saying, "Put your sword away. Would you prevent me from drinking the cup the Father has given me?" Stung by these words, I stood frozen in place while they bound him. John violently jerked my arm and we ran for our lives.

We fled in terror and confusion, having no idea where the others went. When we realized the soldiers hadn't pursued us, we retraced our steps and followed the Lord and his arresters. They took him into Jerusalem to Annas, who shared the office of high priest with his father-in-law, Caiaphas.

John was admitted into the courtyard, since he was known to Annas. I remained outside the gate, crouching in the shadows, afraid of being recognized as a follower of Jesus. A short time later John came out and called, "Peter, where are you?" I emerged from hiding and followed.

As we passed a woman standing by the gate, she said, "Aren't you also one of Jesus' disciples?" I disagreed firmly saying, "I am not."

I disappeared into the crowd gathered in the courtyard, joining those huddled around a large fire in the cold dawn. I listened for news of what was happening to the Lord. Someone said that he was being questioned by Annas.

While warming myself by the fire, one of the temple police who had been at the arrest looked at me intently. I turned my face away. He said, "Aren't you also one of his disciples?" I answered, "I am not."

As I worked my way to the edge of the crowd, one of the slaves of the high priest who was also at the Lord's arrest said, "Didn't I see you in the garden with him?" I denied it vehemently by saying, "I was never there." No sooner had the words escaped, a cock crowed.

What have I done? I thought. *How could I deny my Lord? How could the words of betrayal have been spoken by my lips?* I didn't believe I was capable of such a cowardly act. But, in the end, *I denied him.*

I was devastated by the cowardice of my denials. I, who had sworn allegiance to the death, had crumbled in fear. The "rock" had been crushed; terror had triumphed over loyalty.

The Lord was crucified that same day. I didn't watch . . . I couldn't watch. I was no longer Peter the Rock. In shame, I confessed my new name: Peter the Denier.

Almighty God, who came to show us the way of new life, forgive me when I have proclaimed loyalty with my lips and have denied you with my actions. Strengthen my faith so that it becomes rock-solid when tested. In Jesus' name I pray. Amen.

For Reflection and Discussion

- What is Andrew's role in leading Peter to Jesus? Who has helped lead you to faith in Jesus Christ?
- How does Peter's new name, "Rock," fit his personality as revealed in the scriptures? When have you been "rocky" (stubborn, hardheaded)?
- Would you have allowed Jesus to wash your feet? Why?
- When have you proclaimed loyalty to Jesus, but denied him by words or actions?

Pilate

Read Luke 23:1-25.

Why did I ever agree to come to this godforsaken frontier outpost, far from the comforts of Rome? I hold Sejanus responsible. *He* convinced Tiberius to send me to Judea. How persuasive he was, assuring me that my tour of duty would be temporary. Of course, he also talked Tiberius into taking up residence on Capri, hoping to have the Emperor deposed in his absence. When Tiberius' spies got wind of the devious plot, Sejanus was executed. A man can be too clever.

With Sejanus dead, I will never get back to Rome! I am doomed to waste away my years as procurator of Judea. I hate this desolate land with its torrid, dry days. The dust—it covers everything. I am always sneezing and my eyes water continuously. A dirt cloud hovers over Jerusalem like perpetual fog.

This horrible climate would be bearable were it not for the rabble I am supposed to be governing. Never in the history of Rome has there been a more contentious, unruly, uncooperative, and rebellious race of people. They are always fighting, either among themselves or against us. Ungrateful fools! If it weren't for Roman law, all of Palestine would rapidly degenerate into one colossal riot. Incredibly, they think that we are the problem. They should take a long, hard look at themselves. The Jews hate the Samaritans. The Pharisees hate the Sadducees. The priests hate the scribes. And the Zealots hate everyone! They disgust me . . . all of them.

Within a month of arriving, I had to deal with the first of many protests. Some members of the Sanhedrin were offended by my troops bearing standards with Tiberius' image on them. They sent a delegation to complain that they considered these banners offensive because they portrayed the Emperor as a god. They condescendingly explained that they worshiped only one God and that it was against their law for such idolatrous images to be displayed.

I erupted with outrage! How dare they tell me what my soldiers could or couldn't carry! I had them thrown out! Within hours, the palace was surrounded by hundreds of Jews shouting angrily. I ordered a legion to surround them, but they refused to disperse. Finally, rather than go to war over such a petty issue, I withdrew the troops, agreeing to put another image on the standards. I did not, however, forgive or forget this humiliation.

The next time there was an uprising, I dealt with it severely and quickly. The Samaritans had led an expedition to Mt. Gerizim seeking the tablets of Moses. This caused an uproar among the Jews who believed that Moses received these tablets on Mt. Sinai. I cared nothing for their ridiculous myths. Unfortunately, it was causing such a commotion among the masses, I had to send troops to get them off the mountain. When they refused to leave, I had the fools executed. After that, they thought twice before involving me in their ridiculous squabbles.

A recent problem has been the most explosive of all. On the first day of the primitive festival called "Passover" the entire Sanhedrin burst into my palace like an angry mob, demanding an audience. When I agreed to see them, they shoved a bedraggled fellow in front of me and began accusing him of all sorts of crimes. They said that he was perverting their nation and forbidding them to pay taxes to the Emperor. Then, they got to the heart of their difficulty with him.

"He said that he is the Messiah, the King of the Jews," the high priest shouted with rage.

Why did they involve me, procurator of Judea, in such trivial nonsense? I did not care whether this fellow said he was their Messiah. He could have claimed to be their God and I would not have lifted a finger against him. But, I was curious about what he had to say in his defense.

I asked him, "Are you the king of the Jews?"

"You say so," he answered quietly.

He seemed like a harmless fellow whose only crime had been to offend the Sanhedrin. I didn't believe their charges that he had forbidden them to pay taxes. I would have immediately heard about anyone publicly speaking such treason.

"I find no basis for an accusation against this man," I said. There was no Roman law against claiming to be a Messiah.

The chief priests erupted with a flood of angry allegations against the man they called Jesus of Nazareth. They refused to accept my pronouncement of innocence.

The high priest claimed, "He stirs up the people with his teachings all over Judea and Galilee, where he began his career of blasphemy."

"Is this man a Galilean?" I asked. He slowly nodded his head "yes," suspicious of my motive for asking.

At the mention of Galilee, my spirits rose. That was Herod's jurisdiction. He was tetrarch of Galilee. I had known Herod for many years and we shared a mutual dislike of each other. I seized this opportunity to wash my hands of this Jesus fellow, delighted to turn him over to my enemy. Conveniently, Herod was in Jerusalem for a military meeting. With great relief, I dispatched all of them to Herod.

Imagine my surprise when, two hours later, the Sanhedrin reappeared at my palace with this Jesus fellow. Herod's adviser, who had accompanied the group, privately informed me that Herod had found that Jesus had committed no crime.

95

These Jews were giving me a giant headache, and I wanted nothing more than to be rid of them. I said, "I have examined this man in your presence and so has Herod. Neither of us has found him guilty of the crimes you accuse him of. Therefore, I will have him flogged and released."

You would have thought I had asked them to offer their firstborn sons as human sacrifices! They began shouting and screaming so loudly I covered my ears. Some were shaking their fists in rage. I could not understand how this quiet, self-composed man could pose such a threat.

After several minutes of ranting, their cries merged into a single, ear-splitting chant, "Crucify him! Crucify him!"

I raised my voice above the noise, "Why? What evil has he done? There are no grounds for a death sentence here. I will therefore have him flogged and released."

I feared there was going to be a riot in my own palace court! My guards surrounded me, fearing for my life and their own. Suddenly, I saw a way out of this mess.

I held up my hand for quiet and eventually, the shouts tapered to a low rumble. I said, "Because your holy festival of Passover is about to begin, I will show my generosity as your governor. One prisoner will be released. You may choose either Barabbas, a well-known murderer, or Jesus."

To my astonishment, they shouted with one voice, "Release Barabbas! Crucify Jesus!" They kept shouting louder and louder, until I had to cover my ears again.

Although I didn't want to execute an innocent man, neither could I afford for this disturbance to grow. I could see clearly that nothing less than Jesus' death would quiet them. They were like a pack of bloodthirsty jackals circling an innocent lamb. I debated within myself whether the cost of releasing Jesus would be too high. Roman justice was well known. But, I desired peace more than justice. Besides, what was this Jesus to me? I didn't care to get involved in this family dispute among the Jews. His blood would be on their hands, not mine. If I was ever going to return to Rome, I needed to keep these unruly people under control.

I gave them what they wanted. I ordered the murderer Barabbas released and signed the order for Jesus to be crucified. How much can the death of one solitary man matter, anyway?

Dear Lord, help me to do what is right even when it is difficult. Give me the courage and strength to stand against what is evil and unjust. Remind me that every life is precious in your sight. In Jesus' name I pray. Amen.

For Reflection and Discussion

- What characteristics do you see in Pilate? Which of these do you see in yourself?
- Why does Pilate try to wash his hands of Jesus? When have you tried to shift a problem onto someone else? What happened?
- Why does Pilate finally sign the order for Jesus' crucifixion? When have you wanted to do the expedient thing rather than the right thing? What happened?

Barabbas

Read Mark 15:6-15.

The Romans. The Romans! *The Romans!* To speak their filthy name inflames my rage! Pagans! Heathens! Godless swine with no respect for God's law. I hate them with perfect hatred. I loathe them. Death to every last Roman! Only their destruction will douse the fire of hatred that burns within me.

I am Barabbas. My name means "son of the father" and I am indeed my father's son. He lived strictly by Torah and spent his life fighting those who tried to subvert it. His love of Torah led him to join the Zealot cause long before I was old enough to understand the terrors of Roman tyranny. A leader among Zealots, my father gave everything he had, finally sacrificing his life, in the service of Torah.

He raised me to hate the Roman tyrants who ruled God's land. I learned to abhor their pompous pride and cruel abuses of power. I could not wait until I old enough to join the Zealot cause. As a youth I pledged my life to overthrowing the Romans.

We were called Zealots because of our zeal for upholding the Torah. We committed ourselves to lives of purity and obedience, things the Roman dogs could not understand. How dare the Romans invade the land that the Lord God gave to our fathers! They ignore God's law at their peril!

"Insurrectionists" was the label given us by the Roman pigs, who hated us as much as we despised them. We were at war with the Romans, gladly murdering them to break their hold on God's people. We gave our hearts, minds, bodies, and souls to cutting out the Roman disease from God's land.

I am ashamed to admit that most of my fellow Hebrews were too fearful and timid to join the fight for freedom. They called us "radicals" and worse. We tried to stir them up in a massive rebellion against the Roman despots, but they were cowards. We Zealots had to carry on the rebellion alone.

Ours was a guerrilla war. I organized riots and disrupted the "rule of law" that the Romans were so proud of. Bridges were destroyed, Roman citizens were robbed, and soldiers were murdered. We dedicated ourselves to making the Romans pay dearly for occupying our land.

It was my eagerness to kill Romans that caused my capture. One night, four of us ambushed two soldiers on patrol outside the Jerusalem city walls. As we fought with them, a Roman sword sliced into my leg. We did not know that a Roman battalion was minutes away. When the battalion arrived, I was hobbled by my wound and could not flee.

I lay covered with the blood of a dead Roman soldier facedown beside me. Surrounded by centurions, I knew that I would soon join my enemy in death. I looked up in time to see the flash of a sword above me. I waited for the death blow. Then I heard words that paralyzed me with terror. "Centurion, wait! A quick death is too good for this one. Let's save him for crucifixion."

I was dragged to a dark and squalid Roman dungeon to await crucifixion. From a fellow prisoner I learned that I would be crucified on Passover. As if the agony of crucifixion wasn't enough, I would be put to death in violation of God's law. Although the Torah prohibited executions to be carried out during this holy festival, Roman law made no such exception. What cruel irony! What an outrage!

On the day of my crucifixion a large crowd gathered outside the dungeon window. Because the window was high, I couldn't see what was happening. The noises of the crowd told me that something unusual was going on. I heard my name shouted by the crowd, "Barabbas! Barabbas!" Over and over they shouted my name. My heart pounded with terror. Then I heard the frenzied crowd cry, "Crucify him! CRUCIFY HIM!" The bloodsuckers' screams sealed my destiny. I was to be nailed to a cross.

When the guard came and barked, "Prisoner Barabbas, come out," I was certain that I was taking the first steps up to Golgotha, the "place of the skull." I went prepared to die.

I ascended the dungeon steps into the light of day, my eyes burning at the brightness. As I rubbed them, I felt the shackles being unlocked, first the leg irons, then the wrist chains. I looked around for the heavy crossbeam that I would carry up the hill and saw several in a pile across the courtyard.

The centurion who had escorted me out of the dungeon said through clenched teeth, "Prisoner Barabbas. You may go." I didn't move. "Did you hear me, Hebrew swine? BE-GONE!" I felt a boot slam into my back making me lunge forward. Warily, I walked away, expecting to feel the bite of a sword from behind. I suspected that this was a Roman trick.

No sword fell upon me as I walked to freedom. I had really been released! Once out of the courtyard, I fell to my knees and thanked the Lord that my life had been given back to me. I praised God for letting me live to kill more Romans.

My fellow Zealots found me walking near the palace. They told me what had happened, how Governor Pilate had offered to release a prisoner to appease the unruly crowds gathered for Passover. He had given them a choice: "Shall I release Jesus who is called the Christ, or Barabbas?" The crowds answered "Barabbas" because the chief priests had planted their spies with instructions to shout my name. I wondered what crimes this Jesus had committed.

And so, I was released and Jesus was crucified. My freedom was bought by his death. *So what?* I thought. God must have favored me more than Jesus. After all, I was fighting in a holy war. Jesus was just another criminal.

After a few days, the shock of being free faded. I began to realize that this stranger, Jesus, had died in *my* place. In a way, he had died for me. A question consumed me: Who was this Jesus?

By asking around, I discovered that he had followers who believed that he was the Messiah. They were difficult to find because they went into hiding after their Master's death. Through my fellow Zealots, I was able to locate a few of these disciples who were staying in a house in Jerusalem. At first, they were reluctant to speak with me, fearing that I was a spy sent by the priests. Then one named James told me about Jesus. He said that Jesus was the Son of God who had been sent to save the world. He said that Jesus had healed the sick and had taught about the coming reign of God. He said that Jesus was betrayed, deserted, and denied by some of his closest followers. I was fascinated by James's story.

My fascination turned into wonder when he told me that he and his fellow disciples believed that Jesus had died for them. His death on the cross had given them new lives, he said. He also said that Jesus was raised from the dead by God's power and they had seen him alive.

I left that room feeling like I did when the centurion had told me I was free to go. I was stunned that these men believed that Jesus had died for them. The idea that someone would die for me was overwhelming. The more I thought about it, the more troubled I became. I realized that I should have died on the cross in the place of this godly man. I had murdered without remorse. Women and children had been trampled to death in riots I had incited. I had hurt people and destroyed property. I was motivated by hatred and rage. I did not deserve a second life.

Before I left, James invited me to join them and become part of the rebellion that Jesus had started: a revolution of love. I don't know what I will do. I do know this. Jesus' death gave me a new life. For this I am forever grateful.

Almighty God, who sent Jesus to die for me on a cross, help me to always be grateful for this ultimate act of self-giving love. I receive this gift not as one who is deserving, but as one who is in need. Transform my anger and hatred into the energy of love. In Jesus' name I pray. Amen.

For Reflection and Discussion

• What fueled Barabbas's hatred of the Romans? When have you suffered oppression and what was your reaction?
• How would you react if you were unexpectedly released from a death sentence like Barabbas was?
• How does the knowledge that Jesus died for you have the power to change, even transform, you?
• What do you think eventually might have happened to Barabbas?

The Centurion at the Cross

Read Mark 15:21-39, 44-45.

It was horrible to watch. I had supervised executions before—too many—but none affected me like the crucifixion of the prisoner called Jesus. As an officer in the Emperor's army I have commanded a hundred soldiers in bloody battle. But executions are different; the victim has no defense. The execution of a criminal is cruel, but justified. Killing an innocent man is entirely different. I had to turn my eyes away.

Was it because of the story I had heard about Jesus before fate brought us together on Golgotha?

One of my soldiers told me the story last winter. I was sitting near the campfire, trying to keep the chill away. He had just come off his watch and joined me by the fire. A soldier friend of his, in a different legion from ours, had told him an amazing story about a healer from Nazareth named Jesus. It seems that his friend's centurion (I forget his name) had a slave who became deathly ill. The centurion, having heard about Jesus' skill in healing, sent some friendly Jews to ask Jesus to heal the slave. They did as the centurion asked because he was respected in the town.

As Jesus approached his home, the centurion sent a friend to beg Jesus not to come into his house. He felt unworthy to receive such a holy man. "Just say the word and my slave will be healed," was the message sent. Jesus granted this request and healed this slave without ever coming into the house! Or, so said the soldier by the campfire.

I didn't know what to make of the story. But my knees weakened when I heard that I would be in charge of the execution of the prisoner Jesus. I wondered what he could have done to warrant such a cruel and terrible death. Crucifixion was reserved for the very worst criminals and those guilty of treason. But when Procurator Pilate assigned me to command the crucifixion detail, I followed orders.

From what I was able to learn from talk around the guardhouse, Jesus was being executed because he had said that he was the king of the Jews. I am no lawyer, but I don't know of any Roman statute condemning a man to death for claiming to be a king, unless he were to proclaim himself Emperor. Further, I heard that he was innocent of this charge and that Pilate was caving in to the demands of the Sanhedrin and the chief priest that Jesus be crucified.

It is none of my business whether a man is innocent or guilty. I just follow orders. But, the story of Jesus healing the centurion's slave made me question his guilt.

When we marched the prisoners up the hill for execution, I kept an eye on Jesus. He was barely able to move under the weight of the crossbeam and collapsed facedown in the road after taking two labored steps. The violent flogging he had just suffered had taken its toll.

A man with dark skin was standing by the road watching the spectacle.

"You there. State your name," I ordered.

"I am Simon of Cyrene," he mumbled, his voice shaking with fear.

"Come here," I commanded. He walked quickly. The men of Cyrene knew the sting of a Roman whip.

"Carry this prisoner's crossbeam," I said, pointing to Jesus, who was still lying in the dust. He heaved the heavy beam onto his shoulder and I ordered a foot soldier to help the prisoner to his feet.

Even without the wooden burden, I didn't know if Jesus would survive the hike up Golgotha, the place of the skull. He struggled as if he were still laboring under the weight now carried by the man from Cyrene. I felt moved to help him, but could not break rank. Displays of compassion to prisoners were forbidden.

When the nailers came with their spikes for fixing the prisoners' hands and feet to the cross, I turned away. The sounds of nails piercing flesh and crushing bones were horrible enough, but the cries of agony as the prisoners were hoisted on the crosses always sickened me.

Now lifted, I noticed that Jesus refused the sedative of wine and gall offered to the condemned. It was the lone mercy we allowed during crucifixion. When my soldiers gambled for Jesus' clothes, I didn't join in as I usually did.

After the prisoners were raised on the crosses a parade of mockers filed by, hurling insults at Jesus like stones. "He saved others but he cannot save himself!" one said. Another sneered, "If you're the Messiah then come down from the cross." Even the lowly bandits dying on either side of him joined in the taunts. Finally, I shouted at the bandits, "Shut up! Or I'll add to your pain." *Where were this man's friends?* I wondered. His only supporters were a few weeping women standing at a distance.

At noon a shadow came over the sun and the sky turned black as night. Dark clouds billowed above Golgotha like smoke and the mockers slithered away like snakes. The wind began to gust and dust swirled around us. The soldiers under my command were as skittish as newborn colts.

Then there was an unnatural stillness. In the sudden silence I heard only the labored breathing of Jesus and the bandits. Crucifixion is death by suffocation. Slowly, as a man's strength is drained, he can no longer hold himself up high enough to get air into his lungs. I could tell by the rattle in his gasps that Jesus was nearing the end.

I searched his face for signs of hatred toward those who had mocked him. I looked for a spark of vengeance in his eyes toward his accusers. I strained my ears expecting to hear words of condemnation and rebuke. But no words came from his lips and only anguish lined his face. Then, I saw something else. At first I couldn't believe it was there. But then, it became as clear as the sun on a cloudless day. I saw love. Pity and compassion were etched into the furrows of pain. Jesus, who should have been cursing those responsible for his agonizing death, was silent. And the silence contained forgiveness.

Suddenly, the spell of quiet was broken by a loud yell. Jesus shouted something in Aramaic, a language I didn't understand. A lingering mocker said that he was calling for Elijah, one of the Jews' prophets. Another man fetched a sponge drenched with sour wine, put it on a stick, and ran toward Jesus. I moved to prevent this final indignity being forced on this dying man. Before I reached the stick-wielding man, Jesus cried out loudly and spent his final breath. In that tragic moment I uttered these words: *"Truly this man was God's Son."*

Jesus' final cry still echoes in my mind and in my dreams. I have repeatedly pondered its meaning. Was it a cry of despair, or relief? Was it a final shriek of agony, or a tortured lament? Later, I was told that the Aramaic words Jesus spoke were from a Jewish hymn that begins with the despair of forsakenness and ends with the praise of God. If this is true, then the last cry from the cross was one of triumph. This, at least, is what I believe.

Almighty God, who sent your Son to suffer and die for me on a cross, fill me with gratitude for the self-giving love that was revealed in Jesus' death. Let me proclaim with the witnessing centurion that Jesus was, and is, your Son. In Jesus' name I pray. Amen.

For Reflection and Discussion

- What are the qualities of character displayed by the centurion in this account? Which of these qualities do you possess?
- When have you been caught in the tension between doing your duty and doing what is right? What happened?
- In what ways does the centurion show compassion toward Jesus in this story? What limits his compassion?
- When was the first time you made the faith-statement: "Truly this was God's son"?

Joseph of Arimathea

Read John 19:38-42.

It took all my courage to go to Pilate. As a member of the Sanhedrin, I had participated in audiences with the procurator of Judea several times. I had even been Pilate's guest at a royal dinner along with other leading citizens of Jerusalem.

This time was different.

This time, I wasn't approaching Pilate as a representative of the powerful ruling council. I was going as Joseph, a citizen of Jerusalem.

Walking up the polished marble steps of the procurator's palace, I reflected on how far I had come since leaving Arimathea.

I was raised in the tiny village of Arimathea in the Judean hill country, the son of a simple farmer. As the second-born son, I came to Jerusalem after my father died to make my fortune, while my brother farmed the land he inherited. Quickly recognizing the demand in this great city for luxurious fabrics, I started a business of importing exotic cloth from the far reaches of the Roman Empire.

In only three years I had made a small fortune, therefore earning the respect of some of Jerusalem's wealthiest citizens. My stature in the community led to an appointment to the Sanhedrin. That is where I met Nicodemus.

Nicodemus was a famous rabbi. His grasp of the nuances of the Torah was nothing less than astounding. We soon became close friends, united by a deep devotion to the principles of Torah. Often, we would stay up late into the night debating when the Messiah would come. I argued that the Messiah would come soon, believing God would not let his people live generation after generation under foreign oppressors. Nicodemus disagreed, arguing that the Messiah would come in the distant future, on the Day of the Lord of which the prophets spoke.

Early one morning a year ago, Nicodemus met me wearing a serious expression. He swore me to absolute secrecy before he would tell what had happened.

"Last night I met the rabbi called Jesus," he said.

My face must have betrayed shock. To speak with Jesus without permission from the Sanhedrin was forbidden. Jesus was seen as a dangerous threat to the authority of the council. Some members had called for his arrest.

"Don't worry, Joseph. We met at night. Nobody saw us. The conversation was brief, but confusing. He spoke in riddles and I revealed my ignorance. But I will tell you this: he is a man sent from God."

"Do you realize what you are saying?" I said, worried for my friend. "You could be cast off the council, or worse, for speaking such blasphemy!"

Over the next few months, Nicodemus secretly investigated Jesus. He spoke with people who had been healed by him and interviewed men and women who had heard Jesus teach. He eventually became convinced that Jesus was the Son of God, the Messiah!

At first, I couldn't accept Nicodemus's radical change of heart. I was angry with him and tried to dissuade him from his belief in Jesus. Instead, over time, by listening to my friend's accounts of Jesus' teachings and works, I, too, became a believer.

By the time I joined Nicodemus as a secret believer, it was too late to save Jesus. Caiaphas, the high priest, had convinced the Sanhedrin that Jesus must be stopped. It was only a matter of time before Jesus was captured, tried, and executed.

Subtly using the council's rules, Nicodemus and I tried to turn the Sanhedrin away from taking action against Jesus, but it was an impossible task.

The inevitable tragedy began unfolding early this morning, just past midnight. One of Jesus' own followers betrayed him, delivering him into the hands of the high priest's guards. He was dragged before the Sanhedrin for trial. Caiaphas questioned him, and my appeal for mercy was drowned out by the angry shouts of "Crucify him!" that rang out in the council chambers.

Ironically, Jesus died on a cross as the Passover lambs were being slaughtered. Nicodemus and I sat together in silence while he was crucified. I was in anguish over my inability to stop the raging mob that convinced Pilate to give the order for Jesus' crucifixion.

I realized what I had to do. So I went to the procurator's palace.

My legs were trembling when I reached the doors to the audience chamber. I could see Pilate on the far side of the room, perched on his throne, animatedly gesturing to one of the army of advisers who surrounded him.

After being announced, I walked toward Pilate as if approaching my own crucifixion. I knelt in front of the throne where Jesus had stood only hours before.

"I have come to beg a favor of the procurator, which I pray he will be gracious enough to grant. I would humbly ask His Highness to release the body of the man called Jesus of Nazareth to me for burial. He was crucified today."

Pilate grimaced. "I remember him well. You Jews called for his death, even though he seemed innocent to me. I washed my hands of the whole bloody affair. Why should I give you his body? We usually leave the bodies for the dogs and birds."

"If it might please the procurator, our law says that one who is executed must be buried the same day. Also, if His Highness will indulge me one moment more, this is the Day of Preparation. Our Feast of the Unleavened Bread begins at sundown. If the body is not buried before daylight ends, our law prohibits burial until . . ."

"Don't instruct me about your silly customs!" Pilate thundered. "I will grant your request, not because of your law, but because an innocent man deserves a decent burial."

"Thank you, Procurator. You are most generous. Thank you." Relieved, I bowed low to the floor.

A centurion led me out of the palace and up the hill called Golgotha, the Place of the Skull. The bodies of the crucified lay crumpled in grotesque positions at the foot of the crosses on which they had died. Agonized souls, not yet dead, breathed in gasps. Their cries were haunting.

I was led to a cluster of three crosses. Two men, more dead than alive, hung on the outside crosses. The middle cross was empty. An inscription in three languages nailed to it read: "Jesus of Nazareth, King of the Jews."

The centurion looked up at the two men panting for air. "They'll soon be joining this one," he said pointing to a body lying nearby. "I think this is the one you wanted."

I had only seen Jesus once, from a distance, and the bearded face was unrecognizable to me.

"Is this one Jesus?" I asked a weeping woman standing a few feet away. She looked at me, nodded, and returned to her grieving.

I hoisted the body onto my shoulder (it felt surprisingly light) and started the march to the garden where Nicodemus was to meet me. Even though the burden wasn't heavy, I was moving slowly by the time I reached the garden where the tomb was. The tomb, which I had purchased several months ago as a family burial place, had been completed only a few days before.

As I gently laid the body outside the tomb's opening, Nicodemus emerged from the shadows.

"Is it really him?" I asked.

Nicodemus gazed at the body for several moments. Tears were streaming down his face when he finally said, "Yes, it is the Lord."

"We must work quickly," I said, because the sun was low on the horizon.

Nicodemus walked over to where he had been standing and began dragging a huge sack towards me. I went to help him.

"This weighs at least a hundred pounds. You must have spent a fortune on these spices!" I said.

"Nothing is too extravagant for the Lord's burial," he said.

Silently, we anointed Jesus' body with the lavish amount of spices and wrapped it in the linen cloths Nicodemus had brought. Our tears mixed with the myrrh and aloes as we lovingly prepared Jesus for burial.

When we finished, we carried him into the inner chamber of the tomb and laid a pure, white cloth over his head. Nicodemus rested his hand on Jesus' head for a brief time and closed his eyes in prayer.

Just as the sun was setting, we sealed the tomb by rolling the large, circular stone into the groove hewn for that purpose. It fit perfectly. Nothing will get in here, I thought.

Nicodemus and I walked into the soft light of evening, our arms around each other's shoulders, comforting each other in our loss. It was finished.

Almighty God, give me the courage of Joseph to do what is loving and decent. Open my heart to the good news that Jesus cannot be sealed in a tomb, but is alive forevermore. Raise me to a new life of love, joy, and peace. In Jesus' name I pray. Amen.

For Reflection and Discussion

- In what ways is Joseph courageous in the story? When has your faith helped you overcome your fears?
- Where were you at Jesus' crucifixion? With the women? With those being crucified? With the centurion? With Joseph?
- How was Jesus' burial an act of love? When have you risked yourself in loving actions?

Act IV

Jesus' Resurrection

Mary Magdalene

Read Luke 8:1-3; John 19:25-27; 20:1-18.

The tears are coming more slowly now. I've cried so much these past two days, I can't believe I have any tears left. Each one drips from my cheek and spatters like summer rain into the pool spreading at my feet.

I look into the tomb again. It is lighter and I can see more clearly. I try to convince myself that his body really isn't there. As I lean over, tears fall onto the stone entryway. I want to stop weeping, but I am powerless against the tears.

Peter and John didn't stay long. When I told them the tomb was empty, they ran as swiftly as the wind to see for themselves. By the time I caught up with them, Peter was already inside, handling the burial wrappings. His voice sounded angry, as if he, too, suspected that the Lord's body had been stolen. John said nothing. He smiled as if he knew something Peter and I didn't. They went back to the hiding place.

I am alone. Utterly alone. The Lord is dead. His body is gone, stolen by thieves! Hopeless, I sob tears of anger and sadness.

It is impossible for me to believe that one who was so full of life is dead. I met the Lord a little more than a year ago, yet it seems like I have known him all of my life. He was preaching in Galilee near Magdala where I lived. With the rest of the village, I went out to see this rabbi who was said to be a healer. While listening to the Lord teach, the voices began again. I never knew when they would start. They often came when I listened to the rabbis in the synagogue, or when I prayed.

Those seven voices had been with me as long as I could remember. No one else could hear them. They tormented me for so many years that I gave them names. Lilith (the only female voice). Resheph. Debher. Qeteb. Azazel. Muttalik. Last, but not least, Belial. Sometimes only one spoke. Other times, they all talked at once, sounding like haggling at the marketplace. Whether one or many were speaking, the words spewed forth were of hostility, hatred, fear, and filth. My head felt as if it would burst from the horrible discord. Usually, before the voices ceased I had fainted from the pain.

When the voices started, the Lord looked my way as if he, too, could hear their filthy utterances. As he walked toward me, the voices sounded terrified. They were raging, screaming for mercy by the time he reached out and rested his hand on my head. Jesus' words were drowned out by their wild, shrill wailings. Slowly they faded like echoes. The shock of their silence knocked me to the ground. I grabbed Jesus' feet in joy and gratitude.

From that moment on, I followed the Lord wherever he went. Along with the twelve men, several women were disciples: Joanna, Susanna, and Mary, the wife of Cleopas. Sometimes, Jesus' mother, also named Mary, and her sister traveled with us. Joanna and I gladly donated money we had saved to feed this growing band of disciples.

The year I was with the Lord was the happiest of my life. We never had much food, but whatever we had was enough. We journeyed from town to town, staying as guests of those who invited us. Sometimes, we slept on the ground. It was a hard life, yet fulfilling because we were helping God's Messiah do his work. We were on a mission.

Our mission ended tragically three days ago. The Lord was crucified like a common criminal on the eve of Passover. Just as the lambs were being slaughtered in the temple courtyard for the Seders, the Lamb of God breathed his last.

The women and I, including his mother, watched him die. My heart went out to Mary, who wept bitter tears as her son hung in agony on the cross. I can't imagine the pain of losing a child. Just before he died, he spoke to Mary and John, the only one of the twelve who didn't flee. He looked down on them and said between gasps, "Woman, here is your son. John, here is your mother." And they embraced.

If the crucifixion wasn't humiliating enough, the Lord's burial was indecently rushed. Passover began at sundown, so there was not time to properly prepare the Lord's body. Joseph and Nicodemus hurriedly anointed the body with spices, wrapped it, and quickly laid it in a tomb that Joseph owned. They finished just as the sun was setting.

This morning, when I came to prepare the Lord's body in a way befitting this loving man, it was gone! The stone covering the tomb's opening had been rolled away. The tomb was empty! Not knowing what to do, I ran to tell Peter.

Curse those grave robbers! If they have taken his body they will pay! I pray that the body was moved to another place by friendly hands, safe from those who would desecrate it.

As I look into the tomb, I see two figures dressed in robes so bright that I have to shade my eyes! They are sitting where the Lord's body had lain, one near the head napkin and one at the pile of cloth at the feet. I am so startled my cries grow into wails.

"Woman, why are you weeping?" asks a voice sounding like music.

I stop crying long enough to answer, "Because someone has taken the Lord's body away and I do not know where they laid him."

Suddenly I hear footsteps from behind. I turn my head and see a man. It must be the gardener who cares for the plants and flowers among the tombs. My heart leaps. Perhaps he knows where the Lord's body has been taken!

He asks, "Woman, why are you weeping?"

Ignoring his question, I say, "Sir, if you have carried him away, please tell me where and I will give him a proper burial."

The gardener says, "Mary!"

I turn completely toward this stranger who knows my name. I do not recognize him, but the voice is familiar. Suddenly, it's as if the scales fall from my eyes. It is the Lord!

"My dear Teacher!" I shout. In amazement and joy I fall at his feet and reach out to hold them and kiss them, as I did when he healed me of the voices.

His voice is strong and clear. "Do not hold on to me, for I have not yet ascended to the Father. But rather, go and tell the others that I am ascending to my Father and your Father, to my God and your God."

I rise to my feet and look upon his face one last time. This parting feels like death all over again. I do not understand why I must leave him, but I obey. I turn and walk away. I will myself to not look back like Lot's wife.

My steps become faster and lighter. A breeze blows from behind me, tangling hair around my eyes. I break into a run. Faster and faster I run, as if carried by the wind. Soon I am at the house where the others are. I put my hand on the door and burst into the room, letting in light and wind.

"I have seen the Lord!" I shout. Faces turn toward me in shock, awe, fear, and disbelief. I don't care, so great is my joy. I have seen the Lord! *He is risen!*

Dear Lord, where I expect to find death, you surprise me with new life. Where I expect to discover emptiness, your presence fills me. Where I expect crucifixion to be the final word, you proclaim resurrection. In Jesus' name I pray. Amen.

For Reflection and Discussion

- What does Mary expect to find at the tomb? When have you been surprised to discover new life in death?

- Why does Jesus tell Mary not to hold on to him? When have you had to let go of those you love?
- What is Mary's reaction to her encounter with the Risen Lord? In what ways have you told/showed others the good news of resurrection and new life?

Peter the Rock

Read John 20:1-29; 21:1-23.

My former life seems like a dream long past. So much has happened. So much has changed. No, more than changed—transformed. I, who denied the Lord three times after vowing to follow him to the death, was made into a new man.

The day I denied the Lord was agonizing. After my denial I was immersed in the anguish of remorse. I couldn't imagine denying my Lord even once. Three times was unthinkable, and unpardonable. Instead of standing firm like a rock, I broke, crumbling into pieces like a clod of dirt. Sobs wracked my body. I prayed for death, which would have mercifully ended the pain.

After I denied him, he was taken from Annas to Pilate. The Pharisees and chief priests wanted Jesus to die like a criminal at the hands of the Romans. Later I heard that Pilate interrogated the Lord, asking him, "Are you King of the Jews?" That was the charge the Sanhedrin brought against the Lord. When Pilate found no grounds for execution, he offered to release the Lord as a Passover gift. Outmaneuvering Pilate, the Pharisees incited the crowd to shout for the release of the murderer Barabbas. What cruel irony! A murderer released and an innocent man murdered.

The Lord was flogged, mocked, and crucified at noon on the day of Preparation for Passover. He died quickly, I am told. The Lord's death deepened my wretchedness. I longed to join him in death. Only the love of my fellow disciples saved me. They found me wandering the streets of Jerusalem recklessly, hoping to be recognized and arrested. Andrew led me to a safe house where they were hiding. They fed and cared for me. I was unable to do anything except rehearse my cowardice over and over.

I am told that we hid three days in that home, not knowing our fate. We assumed that the temple police would be looking for us. Hiding in tomblike darkness, we lived in terror of being discovered.

On the third morning one of the women, Mary Magdalene, left at dawn to anoint the Lord's body. Because of Passover, his body had been hurriedly placed in a tomb near where he was crucified. We allowed Mary to go, believing that she would not be recognized as one of the Lord's disciples.

She had been gone less than an hour when she burst into the room while we were eating breakfast. She had been running and was breathless. She came to where John and I were sitting and said between gasps, "They have taken . . . the Lord out of the tomb . . . and we do not know where they have . . . laid him!"

John and I sprinted to the tomb with Mary trailing behind us. John arrived at the tomb first and looked in. "I see the burial wrappings," he yelled. I caught up to him and walked into the inner chamber. There were linen wrappings and also the napkin that must have covered the Lord's head. A new grief took hold of me. Not only had the Lord been crucified, his body had been stolen! This act of defilement enraged me. John and I left Mary weeping at the entrance to the tomb and returned to the house.

Shortly after we returned, Mary exploded through the door again. This time, she was not only out of breath, the color was drained from her face.

Trembling she said, "I have seen the Lord!"

How could this be? I thought. *Hasn't the Lord been dead for three days?* She told of meeting a man whom she thought was

123

the gardener. He asked why she was weeping and she replied that the Lord's body had been taken from the tomb. Then he called her name and she recognized the gardener as the Lord! The Lord then told her to come and tell us, "I am ascending to my Father and your Father, to my God and your God."

We didn't know what to think about such a wild story. John believed Mary. I wanted to believe, but had reservations about the truth of Mary's tale.

It wasn't long before Mary's story was confirmed. That very evening, while we hid in the house the Lord suddenly stood among us. He said, "Peace be with you."

I was certain that his presence was an illusion, until he showed us the nail marks in his hands and feet and the wound in his side. We all rejoiced because it really was the Lord! He had been raised! I searched his face for recrimination but saw only peace.

The Lord said, "As the Father has sent me, so I send you." He breathed on us and said, "Receive the Holy Spirit." As his breath drifted over me, it was like a new spirit began to dwell in me. I felt healed of my grief, forgiven for my denial. I was a new man!

After this we waited. Day after long day we waited. The authorities gave up trying to find us. Rumors of them asking for us stopped. We hadn't seen the Risen Lord for nearly a week, since the day he appeared to Thomas.

I argued that we had waited long enough. "It is time to do something," I said. Five others agreed with me, but five felt that we should wait for instructions from the Lord.

"The Lord may not come to us again. Remember he said that he was ascending to the Father?" I said. We argued about what to do next.

I waited another interminably long day until I couldn't stand being idle a moment longer. I said, "I am going fishing." Six others, including Andrew, came with me.

We walked to the Sea of Tiberias, where I borrowed a friendly fisherman's boat. As it was late in the day when we arrived there, we fished all night, catching nothing.

At daybreak, we noticed a man standing on the shore. "Children, have you no fish?" he yelled. "None," Andrew shouted back. "Cast your net on the right side of the boat and you will find some." We did as we were told.

The net so quickly filled with fish it was in danger of ripping. Then John said, *"It is the Lord!"* I quickly put on my tunic, jumped into the water, and swam to shore, arriving before the others. The Lord was there, standing by a small fire. The others cautiously approached us a few minutes later.

"Bring some of the fish you have caught," he said. I leaped aboard the boat and hauled the net ashore. There must have been over 150 fish! I grabbed a handful of the choicest and returned to the fire.

"Come and have breakfast," the Lord invited.

Not only was I surprised to see the Lord again, I was also embarrassed. I had doubted that he would come to us again. That is why I returned to my former trade: fishing was the only skill I knew.

After breakfast, the Lord motioned for me to walk with him. A short distance from the campfire, he stopped and said, "Simon son of John, do you love me more than these?"

I was puzzled and hurt that he addressed me by my former name. Was I no longer Peter?

"Yes, Lord, you know that I love you."

"Feed my lambs," he said.

He asked me the same question a second time and again I assured him of my love.

"Tend my sheep," he said.

A third time he asked me, "Do you love me?" I passionately said, "Lord, you know everything. You know that I love you." My heart was breaking because he had questioned my love for him three times.

"Feed my sheep," he said.

Then it dawned on me why he had asked three times for reassurance of my love: I had denied him three times. Did the three affirmations of my love for the Lord cancel out the denials? I desperately prayed they did.

The Lord continued, "I tell you truly, when you were younger, you used to fasten your own belt and go wherever you wished. But when you grow old, you will stretch out your hands, and someone else will fasten a belt around you and take you where you do not wish to go." Then he said, "Follow me."

I was perplexed by the Lord's words. Was he saying that I would follow him in crucifixion? Was he asking me to follow him in death now? If he was telling me the manner of my death, I felt no fear. I would not allow the fear of death to cause me to deny the Lord again.

From that day on I put away my nets, never to fish again. The Lord had given me the task of caring for his sheep and lambs. No longer did I dwell on my denials. No more did I wonder how I should serve the Lord. I was made into a new person. Just as God had raised the Lord from death, so had I been raised from the living death of self-condemnation.

In that moment, I reclaimed the name the Lord had first given me. No longer was I Simon the Denier; I was Peter the Rock.

Dear Lord, give me the strength to cope with life's trying times. Just as you raised Peter out of despair over his denial of you, raise me to a new life. Just as you gave Peter charge of your sheep, give me a mission. In Jesus' name I pray. Amen.

For Reflection and Discussion

- Imagine how Peter felt after his denial of Jesus. When have you felt like this?

- How did Peter know that Jesus had forgiven him? What reassures you of God's forgiveness?
- Why did Peter return to his former trade of fishing? When have you felt the pull of going back to what is familiar in a crisis? What happened?
- In what ways can you carry on Peter's ministry of "feeding" Jesus' sheep and lambs?

Doubting Thomas

Read John 11:16; 14:5; 20:24-29.

Thomas is not my given name. Neither is "Doubting," although I am called that also. Thomas means "twin." I am called this because of my twin brother, James. Some people assumed that I was the twin of Jesus because we looked so much alike. Although flattered to be mistaken for the Lord, I always corrected this error.

While I don't mind being called Thomas, I hate having "doubting" added to my name. Why should I be singled out for doubts that any reasonable person would have had?

I was one of the original Twelve called by Jesus as disciples. One day, Nathanael interrupted me as I was working in my father's shop.

"We have found the Messiah! Come and see!" he blurted out.

I rushed out of the shop, following my friend. We came to the outskirts of Bethsaida, where I saw the man of whom Nathanael spoke. As I studied his face I was stunned; it was like looking into a mirror.

When Nathanael introduced me to Jesus, all he said was, "Follow me." You wouldn't think two simple words would be enough for a man to leave everything behind. Incredibly, I followed, leaving behind my parents, my trade, and my home. I never looked back. Are these the actions of a doubter?

As a result of following Jesus, my life changed more than I ever thought possible. Our band of thirteen traveled from one dusty village to another. We had no means of earning a living and often no place to stay. We gleaned what we could from the fields and accepted alms from some of the generous people who were captivated by Jesus' teachings.

Jesus was a master teacher. Though none of us understood all of what he taught, what we did grasp led us to believe that he was the Messiah, the Son of God.

The signs he performed convinced me that Jesus was the Messiah. Each sign revealed a deeper, hidden meaning. Turning water into wine showed that Jesus was the new wine, sent by God to give life to the world. In the healing of the man born blind, I saw that Jesus was the True Light who cures the blindness of unbelief.

The last of Jesus' signs, the raising of Lazarus, was the most mysterious and glorious of all. Instead of rushing to the side of his beloved friend when he first received news of Lazarus's illness, Jesus stayed where he was for two more days. Thinking this strange, we asked him about the delay. He replied, "This illness does not lead to death; rather it has happened for God's glory."

We were terrified when Jesus led us toward Judea, Lazarus's home. Some Pharisees had tried to stone Jesus in the region a few days earlier. When we arrived, Jesus said, "Lazarus is dead. For your sake, I am glad I was not there, so you may believe. Let us go to him."

I said to my fellow disciples, "Let us also go, that we may die with him." For I knew that going deeper into Judea likely meant that Jesus would be killed. We had heard rumors that the Sanhedrin had condemned him as a blasphemer. If they could gather any evidence, even false testimonies, they would have grounds to arrest Jesus and put him to death. Knowing this, I still was willing to follow him. Not exactly the sentiments of a doubter.

After the Lord raised Lazarus, some of the Sanhedrin openly sought to arrest Jesus, afraid of his growing power. We went into hiding.

In the days before his death, the Lord taught us many things to prepare us. One evening he said, "Let not your hearts be troubled." He then spoke of a place where he would soon be going. He would prepare this place for us and take us to it. None of us understood what he was saying, until later. Then he said, "You know the way to the place where I am going."

Bewildered and frustrated, I blurted out, "Lord, we do not know where you are going. How can we know the way?"

A look of compassion crossed his face as he said, "I am the way, and the truth, and the life."

We didn't understand then what he was saying, but we were afraid to ask him questions. It wasn't until his death and resurrection that I understood what he meant. Jesus was the way to a new and abundant life. Those who believe in the Lord commit themselves to follow his "way" of love, compassion, and service.

Our hearts were troubled and afraid when he died. We felt lost, like sheep without a shepherd. We were afraid that we would meet the same agonizing end as Jesus. We hid together in the days after his death, trying to draw strength and comfort from one another. Peter was especially distraught because of his denials of the Lord. Like a dead man, only a faint flicker of life was discernible in his eyes.

For three days, I hid with the others in that shuttered room. On the first day of the week, Mary Magdalene broke the spell of gloom with a fantastic tale of seeing and talking to the Lord. Peter and John went to the tomb, but had only seen the burial cloths. Consensus among us was that the Lord's body had been stolen. John alone believed Mary. The rest of us doubted her story.

It was impossible for me to stay in that awful room devoid of fresh air and light. I felt it was a prison from which I had to escape. I left for a long walk, risking arrest by the temple police. The light and air lifted my spirits. I reveled in the freedom of walking the streets and seeing children playing, women trading at the market and scribes arguing over points in the Torah. When evening came, I forced myself to go back to that grief-filled room.

I used our secret knock. The door opened to a room different from the one I left. Excitement charged through those gathered there. I could have sworn my fellow disciples' bodies had been possessed by different men. The men I left were downcast and depressed; these men were joyful! The men of this morning were defeated and dejected; these men were victorious! I marveled at this.

"We have seen the Lord," Peter, Nathanael, and John said with conviction.

I no more believed them than the story Mary Magdalene had told earlier. I didn't enjoy doubting the word of my fellow disciples, but such a wild tale wasn't believable. Perhaps they had seen a vision of the Lord. Yes, that was possible. I had heard of people losing a loved one and later hallucinating about them. I wanted to believe, but I couldn't bring myself to trust their word alone. They had been confined to this dismal room too long, while I had the clarity of mind that comes from walking in the fresh air.

When they persisted with their story, I finally said, "Unless I see the mark of the nails in his hands and the wound in his side, and touch them, I will not believe."

Should I be condemned for doubting? Their story was beyond belief. I believed in the Lord, but to believe that he was raised from the dead would take more than grief-stricken testimonies. I needed proof.

One by one they turned away, as if I had betrayed them. "I'm leaving," I said, "Will anyone go with me?"

"We'll stay here in case the Lord appears again," they said.

I returned to my parents home, but was restless. I couldn't erase the thought of the Lord appearing to the others from my mind. I felt drawn back to that house where they were staying. Eight days later, I returned.

I forced myself to rap on the door. Again I entered the dark room. The doors were still shut and the windows covered. As I opened my mouth to speak, I felt a presence beside me.

"Peace be with you," a voice said. I turned and saw a vision of the Lord, a vision so real that I found myself understanding how the others could have believed it was the Lord.

The vision spoke, "Come and put your finger here and feel my hands and my side. Do not doubt but believe."

In that moment, I believed that the Lord had been raised from the dead by the power of God! I did not touch him, for all doubt had vanished.

"My Lord and my God!" I said. As quickly as he appeared, he vanished.

Was it a vision or the Lord? It no longer matters. I now believe that the Lord has been raised and lives eternally with God the Father. More important, my belief has led me to follow the Lord's way. In following, I have been raised to a new life.

I have been denounced for doubting. Because I did not have the advantage of the first visit from the Lord on the day of resurrection, am I to be forever cursed? Because I wanted tangible proof that the Lord was raised, is my faith less real?

If I had not doubted, would I have encountered the risen Lord? I do not know. I do know that doubts led me to belief.

Before the Lord left, he said, "Have you believed because you have seen me? Blessed are those who have not seen and yet have come to believe."

May you, who have not seen, be blessed by believing.

Dear Lord, help me to walk not only by sight, but also by faith. With the eyes of faith, may I see your risen presence in daily life. Let me be open to believing the testimony of others who, through faith, know you. In Jesus' name I pray. Amen.

For Reflection and Discussion

- In your opinion, is Thomas a man of faith or doubt? Why?
- In what ways can you identify with Thomas? When have you experienced doubts about Jesus' resurrection?
- How did Thomas' doubts lead him to belief? What kinds of doubts lead to belief? What doubts lead to unbelief?
- How are we dependent on the testimony of the earliest witnesses to Jesus' resurrection?

Two Disciples on the Road to Emmaus

Read Luke 24:13-35.

It was Sunday afternoon. Not just any Sunday, but two days after our Lord, Jesus of Nazareth, had been crucified.

He died like a criminal on a cross of agony. I was still choking down sobs. I kept asking, "How could they have done this to such a loving and innocent man?" He lived a life of compassion and concern for those who were diseased and ill. He healed the blind and lame. He cleansed lepers. He would not even turn away children, encouraging them to come and sit with him. With loving words and deeds, he proclaimed God's coming reign. What a cruel and senseless death.

As his power grew, so did the Sanhedrin's fear. Many times, the temple police tried to arrest him for blasphemy. So great was his popularity with the common people, they dared not lay a hand on him. Throngs would flow out from villages to hear him teach and to be healed by him. In the end one of our own, Judas, betrayed him.

On that Sunday not only was I sorrowful, I was angry. We had been cheated of the Lord's presence. No longer could I sit by his side and hear his amazing teachings. Never again would I gaze upon his bearded face shining with wisdom. Part of me wished that I had been crucified with him.

There was an emptiness inside me, vast as the Negeb, that memories of the Lord could not fill. My spirit was wounded by his death. It was an injury that would not heal quickly.

Deepening my desolation was the reality that our hopes had died on the cross. We believed that Jesus of Nazareth would be the one to lead our nation to salvation and triumph. We had hoped that he was the one God sent to redeem the world. These dreams were crucified with him.

That Sunday morning my heart was as heavy as the pillars of the temple as my fellow disciples and I came together in sorrow and fear. We were hiding from the authorities in a house in Jerusalem. If they could so easily crucify our Lord, they would not hesitate to do the same to us.

Just after dawn, after we said prayers, several women went to the Lord's tomb to properly anoint his body with spices for burial. There had been no time for this on Friday because Passover was beginning. They quickly returned with an astonishing story. They didn't find a body in the tomb. At first they thought it had been stolen. Then in a vision, angels told them that the Lord had been raised from the dead! We listened with open mouths and closed hearts.

I wanted to believe the women's story, but could not bring myself to cling to such a false hope. The others in the room shared my skepticism. We were too mired in the darkness of grief to believe this story of light and life.

I had to escape the gloom of the tomblike room filled with weeping men and excited women. I needed to breathe fresh air and see the light of day once again. I no longer cared about the risk. I asked my friend Cleopas if he would go with me to visit my parents in Emmaus. "It is only seven miles," I assured him. "We can be there in time for supper if we leave now."

A burden lifted from my spirit as I left that awful room in Jerusalem. Leaving felt like the beginning of a new life. I didn't tell Cleopas I was planning to quit the community of disciples and return to being a potter, the trade I left to follow Jesus of Nazareth.

As we walked along the dry and dusty road, we began to discuss the unbelievable story the women told about the Lord being raised from the dead.

"I think the women were telling the truth," he said.

"The truth? How can you believe such a story? The body was missing because it was stolen. It's nothing more than a tale of grieving women seeing what they wanted to see," I said.

"If God wanted to raise our Lord from the dead, don't you believe that he could?" said Cleopas.

"God can do *anything*. But these women were dreaming, I tell you. Nothing more." I was nearly shouting as I spoke.

Our arguing became so heated that we didn't notice the stranger approaching us. Suddenly, he was next to us. He seemed to appear from nowhere, a shadow in the daylight, and asked what we were discussing.

Cleopas and I had difficulty believing that this stranger had not overheard our loud argument. Even so, Cleopas patiently told the story of how Jesus of Nazareth was arrested, tried, and crucified.

I was unhappy with Cleopas' revealing so much to the stranger. *What if he is a spy from the high priest?* I thought. Yet, I did not stop Cleopas from speaking.

To my amazement he even told this stranger the story of the women at the tomb earlier in the day, of how they had seen a vision of angels who said that Jesus had been raised from the dead. He added that some of the men had also gone to the tomb, but saw neither a body nor angels.

Then the stranger spoke in a voice laced with disappointment. "How foolish you are," he said. "How slow you are to believe what Moses and the prophets declared about the Messiah. They proclaim that the Messiah was to suffer at the hands of men and then enter into glory."

He proceeded to teach us from the prophets, beginning with Moses, about the Messiah. He led us through the Psalms and Isaiah, showing us how the Messiah was to suffer and die for the sins of the world. While we walked in stunned silence, I could feel a burning within my heart. He reminded me of someone I once knew.

He spoke for more than an hour, but it seemed like only a few moments. As we drew near to my home village of Emmaus, he turned to walk farther on the road. For some reason, I couldn't bear to see him leave. Panicking at the thought of being out of his presence, I begged him to stay and share supper with us. The day had faded into evening and it was time to break bread. To my great relief, he agreed.

When we arrived at my parents' home, supper was already prepared. In their delight at seeing me, they forgave my bringing two extra guests. They greeted Cleopas and the stranger like nephews.

We sat at the table. Then the stranger, whose name I had forgotten to ask, assumed the role of host. He took the bread, blessed it and broke it. These actions seemed familiar, as if I had seen him perform them before.

Suddenly, it was as if a blindfold had been torn from my eyes. It was the *Lord!* The instant I recognized him he was gone, vanishing as mysteriously as he appeared.

Cleopas and I looked at each other in wonder. He must have recognized the Lord in the same moment. Without taking time to finish supper, or to explain to my parents what had happened, we left for Jerusalem. I didn't care that it was almost dark outside; I felt as if a torch was lit inside me. As much as I dreaded returning to that room of sadness, we were frantic to tell our fellow disciples what had happened.

When we arrived, the dark Jerusalem room had been transformed. I looked at the faces of my fellow disciples, realizing that the fog of grief had lifted. Their faces radiated joy! They greeted excitedly saying, "The Lord has risen indeed, and has appeared to Simon!"

They listened eagerly as we told them how the stranger met us on the road to Emmaus, how our hearts burned as he taught, and how we recognized him in the breaking of bread. They were amazed, but this time, everyone believed.

O Lord, Emmaus is where I flee when hope seems lost and dreams have died. Help me to know that the Risen Lord walks with me. May I recognize him in such common actions as the breaking of bread and sharing the cup. In Jesus' name I pray. Amen.

For Reflection and Discussion

- When have you wanted to flee a painful and disappointing situation? Where did you go?
- How is the Risen Christ with you when you "walk to Emmaus"?
- Why was Jesus recognized in the breaking of bread? Where do you recognize Jesus' presence?

The Beloved Disciple

Read John 13:21-30; 20:1-10; 21:1-23.

We had been fishing all night on the Sea of Tiberias with not even a sardine to show for our efforts. Fishing was Peter's idea. After dinner he jumped to his feet and abruptly said, "I'm going fishing." It was just like Peter: acting before thinking. Not wanting him to be on the water alone at night, I had said, "We'll go with you." The others followed, as they usually did.

This was the first time Peter had been fishing since he was called by the Lord to be one of the Twelve. Like James and John, he and his brother, Andrew, had once been fishermen. I think despair drove Peter back to fishing. The Lord's death had been hard on him. Deepening his grief was guilt over his denials of the Lord during the trial.

Perhaps he went fishing hoping to find comfort in the familiar actions of casting and hauling in nets as well as the fresh smell of the sea. Or, maybe he was thinking about returning to his former trade now that the Lord was dead.

The sunrise was stunning with orange and yellow light dancing off the ripples in the green-blue water. We were taking a long break, having lost our enthusiasm for casting a net only to have it return empty.

I glanced toward the shore and was surprised to see a stranger standing there at such an early hour. The man called out, "Children, did you catch any fish?"

"No," we yelled back. There was something familiar about his voice and the way he called us "children."

The stranger said, "Cast your net on the other side of the boat and you'll catch some."

We did as the stranger commanded, even though there were a few skeptical grumbles. To our astonishment, the net was so full of fish that we couldn't haul it in without tearing the webbing. I wondered to myself, "Who could perform such a sign?"

Suddenly, it was as if the sun rose within me! I realized who the stranger was! "It is the Lord!" I yelled.

Without hesitating, Peter threw on his tunic, dove into the water, and began swimming ashore. This time, he was going to be first.

From the beginning, Peter viewed me as a rival for the Lord's affections. It was obvious that the Lord loved us all. But, he was more outspoken about his love for me. Instead of using my given name, the Lord called me his "beloved." At fellowship meals, I sat closest to the Lord. I always asked the Lord questions the others were afraid to ask. During our final meal together, when the Lord said that one of us would betray him, I was the one who had asked, "Lord, who is it?"

When the Lord was crucified, I remained at the foot of the cross while the others fled. I, and some of the women, witnessed his death.

Before he died, as he hung in agony, the Lord said to his mother, "Woman, behold your son," while his eyes rested on me.

Then, he said to me, "Here is your mother." From that day, I took Mary into my home and cared for her as I did my birth mother.

On Sunday one week ago, when Mary Magdalene burst into the room saying that the Lord's body was missing, I outran Peter to the tomb. I was first to see that the Lord's body was gone. Seeing the tomb empty, I believed that the Lord had been raised, as he said he would, even though I was unsure of what this meant.

We reached the shore soon after Peter, dragging the overflowing net behind us because we couldn't lift it into the boat.

Peter was speaking with the Lord. A fire was burning and bread was sitting on a rock being warmed by the coals. We approached them cautiously.

The Lord said, "Bring some of the fish you just caught."

Before any of us could move, Peter ran and hauled the net ashore.

"There must be over a hundred and fifty fish!" Peter called out.

Peter returned with an armful of the largest fish and the Lord invited us, "Come and have breakfast."

None of us said anything to the Lord. We were not only awestruck, but also afraid. Though I believed it was the Lord, I wouldn't risk asking, "Is it really you?"

It is difficult to describe the confused feelings that were flip-flopping inside of me like the fish on the shore. Yes, I was overjoyed to see the Lord. Seeing him standing on the shore and hearing him speak confirmed that he really had been raised by God's power. It was one thing to see an empty tomb; it was another to see the Risen Lord. Yet, there was a part of me that wondered, "Can this really be true?" I was balanced on the precipice of supreme joy and hesitant hope; teetering between doubt and faith.

In the end, joy and faith triumphed over doubt.

When the Lord blessed the bread and fish and gave them to us, I was certain that it was the Lord, risen and alive. He had performed the same actions when he fed the five thousand and called himself the Bread of Life. During his final meal with us he broke bread and shared the cup.

After breakfast, the Lord walked away a short distance with Peter. I tried to eavesdrop on their conversation, but could only catch the words "love me" and "you know." I could see from the way Peter stood with outstretched arms and upturned palms that he was pleading with the Lord. Peter's tone seemed urgent and distressed, even though the words were unclear.

When they started walking farther away, a heavy sadness enveloped me. I might never speak with the Lord again! I had to follow them.

When I drew close enough to understand their words, Peter turned toward me and said, "Lord, what about him?"

I didn't know what Peter was asking because I hadn't heard what had been said before.

The Lord replied, "That is none of your concern. If I want him to remain until I come, what is that to you? Your concern is to follow me!"

Slowly, it dawned on me that the Lord was talking about his return and my death! Later, I learned from Peter what the Lord had said to him: "When you grow old, you will stretch out your hands, and someone else will fasten a belt around you and take you where you do not wish to go."

Now I am old, and death beckons. Indeed, Peter fulfilled the Lord's word: he was crucified in Rome many years ago. Peter, who wanted so badly to be first, was the first to join the Lord in death.

For years I have puzzled over the Lord's final words to me. He has not returned and I will surely die before he comes. Of course, he did say *if* it was his will that I live until he comes.

My faith in the Lord has taught me that *when* the Lord returns doesn't really matter. The Lord never really left. His Spirit, the Spirit of Love, abides with me and dwells within me. I, who was the Lord's beloved in life, look forward to joining him in death.

Dear Lord, help me realize that I, too, am one of your beloved children. Let me be open to your presence while performing everyday, routine tasks. May your Spirit abide with me so that, in life and in death, I dwell with you. In Jesus' name I pray. Amen.

For Reflection and Discussion

- Why did Peter and the other disciples return to fishing after Jesus' death? What causes you to return to old and familiar ways?
- How did the beloved disciple recognize the Risen Lord? Where do you recognize the Risen Christ in daily tasks?
- What reassures you that the Spirit of Christ dwells within you? What are the signs in the Spirit's indwelling?

Performing the Character Portrayals as Dramas

One possibility for using this book is to allow the characters to speak through you. These portrayals can be performed as dramatic monologues or dialogues in worship and classroom settings. For those who want to venture onto the stage or into the pulpit, I offer the following suggestions.

- Read the portrait aloud several times, trying to capture the character's voice. Walk in the character's shoes, imagining how the character would express himself or herself. If possible, deliver the portrait by memory.
- Decide whether to wear a costume or a simple robe to enhance the dramatic effect.
- For some characters, a prop can add to the dramatic effect. For example, you might hold a staff when portraying "the shepherd boy" or a clay jar when portraying "Mary of Bethany." Be creative.
- When presenting "Mary and Martha," you can perform it as a dialogue with two persons, or as a "one-person dialogue." If you choose the latter, you can distinguish between the characters by turning to one side when speaking as Martha and turning to the other side when speaking as Mary. The same side-to-side technique can work for Mary of Bethany as she moves between past and present.
- Give a short introduction telling your audience that you are going to offer a dramatic monologue. "My name is [character's name]" is all that you will need most of the time.
- If you use a character portrayal as a sermon, decide whether or not you will sermonize about the character. If you do, the questions at the end of each portrait may suggest sermon directions.